MY FORGIVENESS JOURNEY

© 2020 Evelyn Goodman
Printed in the United States of America

All rights reserved. This publication is protected by Copyright, and permission should be obtained from the publisher prior to any prohibited reproduction, storage in a retrieval system, or transmission in any form or by any means, electronic, mechanical, photocopying, recording, or likewise.

Published by Mt. Nittany Press, an imprint of Eifrig Publishing,
PO Box 66, Lemont, PA 16851.

For information regarding permission, write to:

Rights and Permissions Department,
Eifrig Publishing,
PO Box 66, Lemont, PA 16851, USA.
permissions@eifrigpublishing.com, 888-340-6543.

Library of Congress Cataloging-in-Publication Data

by Evelyn Goodman
p. cm.
Paperback: ISBN 978-1-63233-267-7
Hardcover: ISBN 978-1-63233-268-4
Ebook: ISBN 978-1-63233-269-1

1. Memoir—20th Century 2. Memoir—Spiritual 3. Memoir—Travels
I. Goodman, Evelyn. II. Title

24 23 22 21 20
5 4 3 2 1
Printed in the USA on recycled paper.

MY FORGIVENESS JOURNEY

Changing My Destiny
As I Traveled Worlds

A Memoir

Evelyn Goodman

LEMONT

Forgiveness is everything.
When I think of forgiveness
I am brought to weep with
Gratitude that it exists.

Maya Angelou

Dedication

*To the Blessed Memory of the Hasidic Master
Rebbe Levi Yitzhak of Berditchev,
my great-great-great grandfather,
and
To my Guru, the manifestation of blessings in my lifetime*

For my beloved family

Contents

Part 1
Life Before Awakening

1	Beginnings	13
2	Childhood	16
3	Blossoming into Adulthood	19
4	Teaching - Heart to Heart	21
5	A Tale About a Fairy Tale	33
6	Anticipating the Big Day	35
7	The Wedding	36
8	The First of Many	38
9	Babies – It's Not All Smooth Sailing	40
10	Picking Up the Pieces and Building a Future	53
11	Europe Here We Come	65
	Bullfight	69
	Madrid	70
	Andalusia	72
	La Costa del Sol	77
	A Bump in the Road	79
	Paris	83
	England	85
	Going Home	92
12	Back Home to the Real World	93
13	The Secret Ingredients in the Turkish Delight	94
14	Greece – The Land of Gods	98
15	Keeping My Promise	102
16	The Sweetest Sixteen	104
17	Whispers of Freedom	106
18	The Far East Beckons	107

Part 2
The Forgiveness Journey

19	Initiation	109
20	The Awakening	112
21	The Challenge	119
22	Forgiveness—What It is and What It is Not	120
23	First Steps	122
24	On the Road	124
25	An Eerie Night	126
26	Language of the Heart—The Whales of Baja	127
27	The New York Marathon	130
28	Radiance	132
29	Thanksgiving's Unexpected Goodies	135
30	Height / Weight	140
31	Still on the Road—Further Along?	142
32	The Efficacy of the Mantra	143
33	Alaska	145
34	Representing the Older Women's League Before Congress	154
35	Addendum to Testimony	155
36	The Book Party	156
37	The Road Gets Shorter	158
38	My Three Bat Mitzvahs	160
39	Ashram Moments	168
40	Vienna	170
41	How the Hunter Schools Were Saved	172
42	Getting the Boys Into Hunter High	177
43	Cuba	181
44	Between Two Passovers	183
45	A Healing Meditation	186
46	India	187
47	Thoughts on Meditation	189
48	My Crowning Achievement—Clara N.	190
49	Meeting Bat-E	193
50	The Divine Messenger	194
51	God Sometimes Uses A Plane	201
52	Thanksgiving 2014	204
53	Krakow and Auschwitz	206
54	The End of One Journey	210

55	The Yale Test	211
56	Reaching the Promised Land	215
57	Explaining the Inexplicable	219

Part 3
A New Beginning

58	What Now?	220
59	A Perfect Day in an Imperfect Month	223
60	Mt Sinai	226
61	Silent Retreats	228
62	Pure Love	229
63	Another Perfect Day	231
64	Unexpected Blessings	234
65	Scary Can Be Fun	236
66	The SAJ Spring Retreat	238
67	Double Blessings	240
68	We Can Bless Each Other	242
69	Shabbat Comes Early	244
70	Down Under	246
71	Queen For a Night	251
72	Mystery of Miracles	255
73	Silence Gave Way to Song and It Was Spring	263
74	How Forgiveness Worked For Me	265

Photographs	266
Epilogue	281
Origins of the Back Cover Image	283
Note from the Publisher	284

Foreword

We are dealt a poker hand at birth, and in the game called life we play out our hand. Mine was one I would never have chosen. But destiny, being what it is, gives us no choice.

My travels took me as far from home as Tibet and as close to home as my heart.

This is the story of my journey from far to near, from hurt to healing, how reluctantly I took destiny head-on and much to my surprise, through forgiveness, changed its course.

I hope my story inspires others to do the same.

If I can do it, anyone can.

~Evelyn Goodman

Part I

Life Before Awakening

1
Beginnings

It all started in a *cheder* (school room) in the Ukrainian *shtetl* (small town) of Lipovitz at the turn of the 20th century with a teenage boy named Nechemia Zuzia Tevorovsky. He, along with the other Jewish boys in town, was taught by men who were hardly scholars or passionate about teaching. Rather, they were ordinary men, some barely educated and others cruel, who took on teaching merely as a way of supporting their families.

One day, Nechemia, an inquisitive young boy of almost 13, asked the teacher in Yiddish, the *mamaloshen*, (everyday language) of Jews.

"*Tzis takkeh a Gut?*" (Is there really a God?)

The teacher replied with a hard smack across his face.

"*Azoy min frage frekt min nisht!*" (Questions like that you don't ask.)

With the answer still smarting on his cheek, Nechemia went to the barber and said, "Cut off my *payes* (forelocks).

The surprised barber replied, "I can't do that without your parents' permission. And besides, you have no money."

"Cut off one. I'll be back tomorrow with the money."

That young agnostic became a gymnasium student (equivalent

to high school and some college.) He grew to manhood, became an atheist, and at age 22, left five sisters and a mother behind, and headed for America to an uncle in Falmouth, Kentucky. He married and became my father who raised me to be an atheist.

My mother Rachel Borko, on the other hand, came from an illustrious rabbinical family. Her great, great grandfather was the revered Hasidic master, Rabbi Levi Yitzhak of Berditchev. She too was a gymnasium student, which was a rarity for a Jew, let alone a woman. When her mother died, Rachel, a soft-spoken, shy, reserved, beautiful young woman of 22, became an orphan and was forced to emigrate all alone to America.

On the journey, she, like all immigrants, had to wait for a visa in Bucharest, Romania. There she met the charming, young, handsome, red-headed, curly-haired Nechemia. They fell in love and were married a few months later in Rock Island, Illinois at the home of her sister Manya (Mary).

They left Rock Island, looking for the *Goldena Medina*, (golden land of America, an immigrant belief that the streets of America were paved with gold.) My father, educated and from a middle-class family, had no trade, unlike many of the immigrants arriving at that time—the tailors, shoemakers or bakers. He couldn't make a living as these tradesmen did. But these people, whom he looked down on as being beneath his social class, became successful; he did not.

After a time of wandering around the United States, my parents almost settled in Lincoln, Nebraska, but luckily for me chose Chicago instead. I was born there in 1928. When I was six months old, my four-year-old brother Norman died of a burst appendix and I became their too-precious only child. Dissatisfied with the brutal winters and being far from family, my parents finally decided to settle in New York to be near my uncle Misha (Murray), my father's brother.

My uncle worked as a presser in a sweatshop ironing dresses, and he taught my father the trade. My father had ambitions of becoming a lawyer and went to night school for a while. But the pressures of making a living and taking care of the family were too strong and he dropped out. The closest he got to his dream of being a lawyer was to become the union shop steward of the ILGWU (International Ladies' Garment Workers' Union) in the dress factory where he worked. My father was very hard-working but couldn't make it in our society. He became an angry, frustrated, disappointed man who thought of himself as a failure.

2
Childhood

I grew up in the *shtetl* of Brooklyn in the ghetto of Brownsville. The houses in Brownsville were four-story tenements, much more livable than the overcrowded Lower East Side, built with large back courtyards instead of dark airshafts. Each apartment was heated, had hot water and a toilet. There were seven apartments to a floor and almost all had children living in them. In my building alone, 207 Amboy Street, I once counted about 40 children ranging in age from 4 through 18.

The street was teeming with people but nowhere near the density of the fabled Lower East Side, with its pushcarts, looking like an outdoor bazaar. The only stores were on the corners: the candy store and Wexler's grocery store were on my corner of Blake Avenue; Rosner's grocery store and a deli were across the street. On the other end of Amboy Street, on the Sutter Avenue corner, were a dry goods store, a bar and a *shtiebel*, (a small shul).

Growing up in Brownsville, I thought the whole world was Jewish. Except for my classmate and friend Helen Kolesnik, who was Russian Orthodox, the daughter of a janitor and the only Christian in my class, the whole world *was* Jewish.

The kids were called by Jewish names, like Chayke, Chaya, Mendel and Heshie, as well as more Americanized names like Sammy, Irving, Morris and Abie.

Although there was *Yiddishkeit* (Jewishness) in my home, there was no religion. My father ate on Yom Kippur, the holy day of fasting. On Passover, he ate bread, when bread was forbidden. We didn't have a seder, the meal celebrating the Israelites' freedom from bondage in Egypt. My father, who was not on good terms with his brother and rarely saw him, said, "We have no family. Why make a seder just for the three of us?" When I was 13 and insisted on a seder, we had one but he ran through it quickly and without meaning. I liked it anyway.

My mother observed the holidays, fasted on *Yom Kippur*, ate only matzo on Passover, and sometimes prayed alone in a corner of a room. In 1941, I already knew terrible things were happening to Jews in Europe. They were being killed for being Jews and I began fasting in their honor. My father fasted out of respect for me until I stopped at age 18, at which point he said, "Thank God you finally stopped."

My mother told me a few stories about being a descendent of the Berditchever Rebbe. Her grandmother, Sura Beila, used to wear an apron with the words, "*Ayn Enikel fun der Berditchever*" (a granddaughter of the Berditchever) embroidered on it.

My mother's father, Nucham, was also a revered Rabbi. They lived in the town of Bar, near Berditchev. Although he chose not be a pulpit rabbi, the townspeople came to him for advice because he was wise, compassionate and a descendent of the Berditchever.

My grandfather allowed my Aunt Manya (Mary) to sit in the house with her intended, my Uncle Velvel (Bill), on *Shabbos* (the Sabbath) even after the *Shabbos* candles burned down. He also allowed his daughters to smoke if they wished, but only in the house.

My mother told this story about the Berditchever. When my grandfather died, my mother had to leave gymnasium and go home to take care of her mother. They lived in a large house with a not-so-kind aunt. One day the aunt announced she was closing on a deal to sell the house, which meant my mother and grandmother would have no place to live. They traveled to Berditchev to the Rebbe's grave and as is the custom, put a kvitel (a petitionary prayer) on the gravestone asking for help. By the time they returned home, the deal had fallen through. Their home was saved.

My father pooh-poohed these stories. To him it was all superstition. I had no idea how important the Berditchever Rebbe was in Jewish history. I didn't know that he was, next to the Baal Shem Tov, the most well-known of the Hasidic Rebbes. Because of his compassion, he was also most revered and beloved among the people. My father didn't tell me about Hasidism and what that movement meant to the Jews of Eastern Europe in the 18th and 19th centuries. I knew next to nothing of my heritage.

I didn't go to Hebrew school. I wanted to go to a Bible class given at the Hebrew Educational Society (HES, the neighborhood settlement house) but my father said we couldn't afford the 25 cents. We were poor and I believed that then, but now I think that was just an excuse to keep me close. He did, however, teach me the Yiddish alphabet, how to write my name in Yiddish and how to read from the Yiddish newspaper, the Jewish *Daily Forward.* My parents spoke Yiddish to each other, Russian when they didn't want me to understand and, because they wanted to learn English, they spoke to me only in English. I spoke to them in English and although I understood Yiddish, I never had a chance to speak the language.

I remember running around the synagogue with the other children on *Simchas Torah* (the holiday celebrating the Torah) carrying a flag with an apple on it. I got new clothes in the spring for Passover and for *Rosh Hashanah,* the New Year.

That was the extent of my Jewish education.

3
Blossoming into Adulthood

In 1944, at age 16, I felt very grown up as a freshman at Brooklyn College, where it was fashionable to be an atheist. The next choices were between becoming a Marxist or a Freudian and whether to be in psychoanalysis. If you weren't in psychoanalysis, people thought there was something radically wrong with you..

I chose to be a Freudian and an atheist who, if anyone proved to me that God existed, would go to *shul* (synagogue). My mind was open but I didn't call myself an agnostic. To me, agnostics were cowardly atheists. I was an open-minded, devout atheist who lived in a world of atheism. My friends, boyfriends and future husband were all atheists.

I did not miss a God I did not know.

And yet the universe was too perfect to be a mere accident. If there was a God, I conceded, then He/She created the world but then withdrew without meddling in our petty lives. He/She was too busy; we were too unimportant. Years later, someone responded to that remark saying, "God already did the hard work of Creation; what else does He/She have to do except be involved in our lives?"

I also jokingly believed there must be a "Baby God," for without cosmic protection, it would be a near impossibility for children to grow up in this dangerous world.

God did not enter my life, nor did religion, but I was very much a Jew, a good Jew. I identified strongly as Jewish. I supported Israel, treated people kindly, gave to charity, was involved in politics and wanted to change the world. I did things I felt were morally right, not out of fear of God or the law, but because it was intrinsically the right thing to do.

Upon graduating from college at age 20, majoring in psychology, I wanted to go to graduate school and become a clinical child psychologist, but I was torn between two loves. I didn't want to go out of town for a graduate degree and be away from Phil, my childhood sweetheart, whom I wanted very much to marry. Instead, I chose to get a job teaching nursery school in Bed Stuy and went to school at night in the prestigious City College psychology program. After finishing one semester, I found I had too much on my plate and dropped out of the graduate program.

4
Teaching—Heart to Heart

I student-taught in Williamsburg, an impoverished ghetto in Brooklyn, at the first Hebrew Day Nursery School in the two- to three-year-old group.

Curled up on an empty bookshelf was a little two-and-a-half-year-old boy. He had come from Puerto Rico to this country a few weeks before and had been in school only a few days. He climbed on the shelf and refused to come down, except for food. Without talking to anyone, he gobbled down his food and quickly scrambled up again before anyone could stop him.

I thought I'd give it a try. I walked by during the morning singing "*La Cucaracha*" in Spanish, loud enough for him to hear me. After three or four times I called him by name and said, "*Pedro, quiere aprender Espanol.*" ("I'd like to learn Spanish").

"*Quieres ensenarme Espanol?*" ("Will you teach me Spanish?") And if you want, I said in Spanish, I'll teach you English." At first he didn't answer, but after a while he turned his head, hesitatingly climbed down and without a sound allowed me to take his hand.

I chose my first teaching job in Bedford-Stuyvesant, an impoverished Black ghetto, at the Fredy-Riis Day Care Center, which had an all-Black staff. They were well-educated teachers, graduates of Spelman and other fine Southern schools for Black women who nevertheless came to school with the conservative newspaper, *The Daily News*; I came with the progressive *PM*. They surprised me by saying it was easier for Black people to live in the South as long as they followed the rules. Up North, they could get into trouble because they didn't always know how to act in every situation.

The director, Lovey Nutter, an American, was romantically involved with a man claiming to be a Nigerian prince, who offered me a summer job teaching in his country. I immediately accepted, but that's a story for another chapter. Ninety percent of the children were Black; I was the only white teacher and was assigned to the two- to three-year-old group as an assistant teacher. Many years later, this program came to be known as "Head Start."

Until college, I had very little experience with African Americans. When I was young, in Brownsville, a Black man would come into the backyard and, in a beautiful baritone voice, sing Yiddish songs. The housewives would throw pennies wrapped in newspaper out the window in appreciation.

In junior high school, I met my first Black peer, Shands Chapman, who was in my rapid advancement class. She was smart, pretty, affable and had a beautiful singing voice. When our class performed the operetta *"Hansel and Gretel,"* she was cast as Gretel. She was popular and was voted class president.

Unfortunately, my last experience growing up was not as sanguine. A group of Black teenage girls ganged up on me and my friends while we were in Highland Park, shouting they came from Harlem to beat up on white kids. I was the slowest runner and was the one who got hurt—not so much physically as emotionally.

Learning was a two-way street. My preschool children learned that not all white people were to be feared and some could actually be loved. I learned about ingrained racism and the children's deep fears.
One of the songs I taught them was:
Remember your name and address
And telephone number too
And if some day, you lose your way
You'll know just what to do
Go up to the kind policeman —

With that I was interrupted by a three-year-old tugging at my skirt, who said,

"Him hit people."

Some lessons I shall never forget. I understood viscerally for the first time how destructive and corrosive systemic racism was. Together, the big lesson the children and I learned was that opening your heart to love drove away fear.

Charlie was a two-and-a-half-year-old with a sweet smiling face, a cleft chin, dimples, buckteeth and bright shiny black eyes. He wore shoes that were too big for him, stuffed with paper which made him walk pigeon-toed. His clothes were hand-me-downs, and he was a hand-me-down to us for the entire day. He came at 7:30 AM in time for breakfast and was picked up by his mother at 7:00 PM after snack time at 6:30.

His mother was not married to his father, who was in jail. He lived with his mother and her parents, devout Italian Catholics who condemned her for having a bastard.

Charlie had a dirty mouth; his favorite word was f—- which I gradually got used to after some discomfort. He was a handful, a delicious handful, but a handful nonetheless. I adored him.

The school, located in the projects, used the project playground for its outdoor play time. One day, when our time was up, I called out, "It's time to go back to school." Charlie was standing on top of the slide. He looked down at me and shouted for everyone in the playground to hear, "You f—-." I blushed, feeling like a parent whose child had just badly misbehaved. What would the parents sitting on the benches think? We were a new school and still had to prove ourselves to the community. After his cry of defiance, Charlie slid down, walked over to me, took my hand and quietly walked back to the classroom.

A few days later, Charlie's mother told me they were going on vacation without telling me where and for how long. I was happy for her. She came back after a week. She told me she had lost her job, her parents had tossed them out on the street and that she and Charlie had slept on a park bench.

For years I thought about Charlie and wondered what became of him and his mother. I would look at Page Six of the *Daily News*, which reported local news and gossip. One day to my horror, I read that Charlie's mother had thrown herself off the Brooklyn Bridge. To this day I wonder what happened to Charlie.

Earl was a two-and-a-half-year-old, chocolate brown, cheerful, adorable, happy child who came from a stable home. His mother was in nursing school and his father was a bus driver. With their schedules they needed full-time day care for Earl.

Earl and I bonded; we adored each other. At nap time he would call out, "Evalum, come shake me." I would go to his cot and rub his back until he fell asleep. The director would come by and see me and say, "Boy, he sure does have you wrapped around his little finger." Maybe so, but I felt a little extra attention couldn't hurt—not at two-and-a-half.

One day, on a Saturday afternoon, I was riding in the back of a trolley car with my friend Dolores and a Black male friend of hers. This was New York City in 1949 and people's heads turned when they saw a white woman with a Black man. All heads on the trolley turned again when a little Black boy—Earl—broke out of his mother's arms and ran to the back of the trolley and into the arms of a white woman, shouting, "Evalum."

Ralph W. was a tall-for-his-age, thin, wiry Black three-year-old. He, along with his older brother and sisters, was being raised by a single mom who was doing a Herculean job of keeping her family intact.

Ralph was a handful, a strong, intelligent, active child and a charmer with an excessive amount of energy. When I would sit on the floor and from behind was hugged so hard I was pulled over, I knew it was Ralph. I adored Ralph.

Three very different little boys, all of whom I loved.

Ralph was also someone I wondered about, but with a name as common as Ralph W. it would be hard to trace. He had strong leadership qualities. Would he become a solid, successful member of society, perhaps a leader in the Civil Rights movement, or a leader of a gang? He could go either way.

Forty years later, in 1989, I was working at The Division of Human Rights at the Westchester County office as a Human Rights Specialist investigating cases of discrimination. Part of the duties of an investigator was to answer the phone because we, as professionals, had to make an initial decision about whether a caller had a possible case of discrimination.

One day, my colleague, Florence, asked me to take her shift. I got a call from a man who claimed he was being overlooked for a promotion because he was Black. He trained white people who were eventually promoted, while he was not.

I told him, "Yes, you have a case. Make an appointment and come in to file."

I asked his name.

"Ralph W.."

I couldn't believe it.

"Where did you grow up?"

"Brooklyn."

"Are you about 40?"

"Yes."

I got excited, "Did you go to nursery school in the projects?"

"Yes."

"Ralph," I said incredulously, "I think I was your teacher,"

"I can't remember."

"I'm Evelyn and I think I was your teacher. We'll talk more when you come into the office." I was excited and couldn't wait to see him.

A handsome, well-dressed, smiling young man walked into my office at the appointed day and time. He didn't recognize me but I was sure he was my little Ralph. We talked for about ten minutes when he said, "I recognize you now. I recognize you by your smile."

I asked to be filled in about his life, and he said, "I made it through the projects. I graduated from high school and went into the Navy. I had various jobs and am now working for a large well-known bank."

"Did you ever marry?"

"No, my mother worries about that," he smiled. I could see he was still a charmer.

I asked about his mother and siblings, and he said, "I'm surprised you remember."

I said, "Of course I remember. You were special to me."

I took him around the office, introduced him to my co-workers as my Ralph W. and excitedly told them the story.

I was thrilled, but then we got down to business.

The hardest cases were the ones where people had jobs. If they filed a complaint they took the risk of being fired. Yes, the division could file for retaliation, but in the meantime they'd lose their jobs.

Ralph was loath to file, but I came up with an idea. "Tell your boss about this amazing meeting you had with your nursery school teacher who is now working for Human Rights. When you told her of your situation with the bank, she told you that you had a good case. You don't want to file a complaint; all you want is the promotion that is now open."

Ralph agreed it was the way to go. We waited a few weeks, but again the promotion was given to the white guy he had trained. We had no recourse but to go ahead with the complaint.

I tried very hard not to rock the boat and became friendly with the bank's lawyer who promised to help adjudicate the case.

Months went by with no resolution; I told Ralph these things take time. As we were about to reach a settlement and get Ralph the next open promotion, he disappeared. The bank called to say Ralph had quit work and left no forwarding address. I was disappointed and not having heard from him, reluctantly closed the case.

About a year later, Ralph called to tell me, "I couldn't take the pressure and left for California. I'm sorry. Thanks for everything."

In 1950, armed with a permanent license to teach in the New York public schools, I was assigned to a kindergarten class at P.S.157 on the outskirts of Bed-Sty. It was near the Brooklyn Navy Yard and a Hershey's chocolate factory from which wafted a delicious sweet smell when school was over at three o'clock. This neighborhood was different; mostly Italian, many newly-arrived Puerto Ricans and interspersed with a sprinkling of Blacks and Jews. My co-teacher, Rose Lovely, and I each had a class of 54 children, five- and six year-olds in the morning, and four- and five-year-olds in the afternoon. I chose the afternoon. Rose, age 65, unfortunately wanted to retire, slept through most of my afternoon session, and wasn't much help.

It was a challenge.

Johnny, or Juanito, as his mother called him, age four, was a cross between Charlie and Earl. He came from a stable background, looked as sweet as Earl, but had a mouth like Charlie. By this time, I was used to the f-word, but with so many children around, it was harder to ignore.

Monsita, age five, my mainstay, came up to me, "Miss T. (I wasn't married yet), Johnny said a curse." I turned around to see Johnny with his mouth pursed, ready to say the word. I had to deal with it.

"Monsita, you are such a big girl, I want to tell you a teacher's secret."

She smiled, feeling oh-so-grown-up and self-righteous.

"Johnny wants us to make a big fuss over him saying a curse, but if we just ignore him, we can show him he's not important."

She nodded as we walked away together.

Johnny never cursed again.

One day Johnny's mother came to school, hysterical. Johnny had not come home from school.

"He was absent all afternoon," I told her.

"I left him and his cousin, Maria, in the schoolyard."

"He never got up to the classroom." I became just as worried.

While we were deciding what our next step would be, Johnny and Maria sauntered into the schoolyard. At age four, they had decided to go to Prospect Park and follow the trolley car tracks all the way to the park. When they got hungry, they went back the same way they came—a four-mile roundtrip.

Johnny's mother was too relieved to hit him.

Monsita was smart. She scored 110 on the Stanford-Binet Standardized Test given to five- and six-year-olds. For most children, 110 was average, but that was considered smart for kids with little or no enrichment at home. One of the questions was to identify objects; one object was a five-pointed star. Instead of saying, "Star," the correct answer, Monsita said, "Tip Top Bread." The star was the logo on the bread she ate and food meant a great deal to her. I reluctantly had to mark her wrong.

The teachers were assigned to yard duty as well as to classes. I was 22 and looked 16. Behind my back the 11- and 12-year-old boys would say filthy things to me in Spanish. I pretended I didn't understand and told the principal. When nothing was done to correct the situation at the top, some of the male teachers changed duties with me.

One day, Frankie called Nat the "N-word." Normally, I ignored their use of dirty words, or as they said, curse words. But I would never ignore the use of the "N-word." I said to Nat rather sternly, "That's a word we don't use ever."

He replied, "But I'm Black, I can say it."

"No you can't, not in my class. Never!"

The little ones told their older brothers in the school, "Her a nice teacher." Those older brothers would "casually" meet me at three o'clock and walk me to my trolley car.

Clarissa, age four-and-a-half, usually an active child, was quiet and sat by herself. I went over to her and asked, "What's the matter?

Are you okay?" She told me that the man who used to live with her and her mother was coming out of jail. He was there because he abused Clarissa and was coming back to live with them.

I was a teacher who dared make house visits. It wasn't safe, but I did it anyway. Evita would fall asleep every day in class and when I went to her home I found out why. There were rats in the apartment and rat poison was used to kill them. The rats would eat the poison and go back into the walls where they would die. The stench, which was awful, and her fear of getting bitten, kept her from falling asleep.

Children from Puerto Rico did not know of or have a need for snow suits until they came to New York. Some parents couldn't afford a snow suit. During one storm, I bought one for Norina, whose mother had three other little ones. At Christmas, I got a note with my most treasured present ever:

"Thank you for Norina snow suit," and wrapped in Christmas paper was a can of peas and carrots.

The class was made up of Puerto Ricans, Italians, Blacks, and the one Jewish boy, David Goodman. The children were having a conversation about religion.

One child said, "I'm Catholic."

Another said, "So am I."

A third one turned to David and asked, "What are you?"

He said, "I don't know," and he looked at them blankly.

"What do you mean you don't know? What are you?"

"I don't know."

"I'm Catholic. She's Catholic," pointing to her friend. "Are you Catholic?"

He repeated sadly, "I don't know."

Listening to them, I vowed that even though I didn't believe in God, any children of mine would know they were Jewish and be proud of it.

P.S. 175 was very different, a middle-class school in a safe, clean neighborhood in Forest Hills, Queens, and not a Black face to be seen. The children were different but really the same: needing love, giving theirs with pure hearts and open to learning.

My teaching partner, Mary Gordon, was different from Rose Lovely. She didn't sleep, but instead threatened to report me to the Board of Education, because I didn't have my children say the Pledge of Allegiance every morning. It was the 1950s, the time of the Senator McCarthy hearings and the anti-Communist, anti-liberal witch-hunt. To me the Pledge was too important to be mangled by five-year-olds who didn't understand its meaning. They would be like the children who said their catechism by rote, and thought "The cross I'd bear," was a cross-eyed bear.

I taught them about Sputnik, rockets, and space travel, a far cry from Bed-Stuy, where, when I put pre-reading signs around the room—window, door, desk, book, I was reprimanded by a Board of Education supervisor for teaching the children to read.

Richie reminded me of Ralph—tough but short and stocky—who got into frequent fights. Billy was one of his victims. I wanted to help Billy learn to defend himself and so quietly told him it was okay to break the class rule of no hitting, and to hit back. Unfortunately, Richie overheard our conversation. Soon afterward, Richie was in another fight. When I asked him what happened, he said, "I hit him back first."

Fred was small, did not have social skills, but was extraordinary for a four-year-old kindergarten child. He could read the New York Times. Along with my helping him make friends with his peers, I would send him to a fifth grade class where he would read the newspaper to the ten year-olds.

And then there was Cori. She was a blonde, blue-eyed, bright, effervescent, compassionate child. If someone was sad, Cori would be there to comfort them, not because she wanted to be liked (she was by all the children), but because she truly cared.

Cori's mother, Roz, was my class mother. She took beautiful pictures of the class, and I encouraged her to develop her skills. Her love of photography spurred her on and she became a very successful children's photographer. We became close friends.

Outside of school, Cori called me Evelyn. But during class, she called me Mrs. Goodman, never once slipping, and kept our relationship a secret from her classmates (quite a feat for a five-year-old.) Although the family moved to Los Angeles, Roz, Cori, and I remained friends through the years. Recently, I visited Cori, now age 72, in Los Angeles. When she introduced me to her grandchildren, "Evelyn was my kindergarten teacher," they were incredulous. Cori hadn't changed. She still cares about people and tries to make the world a better place.

I would take the class on field trips around the neighborhood. Among them was a visit to a local florist. One girl said to her friend, "Don't look so hard. She'll make you draw about it when we get back."

When I asked them where milk came from, and they said "supermarket," I knew it was time to take the class to an animal farm. We were greeted by a peacock, preening, showing his beautiful feathers. I asked, "Is that a male or female? "

All the children shouted out without hesitation, "A female."

They were very surprised to learn that in the animal kingdom the male is more attractive than the plain unadorned female.

We had a Museum of Unnatural History. The children drew imaginary animals, gave them a name, species, habitat and food. It was fun to decorate the walls with these animals.

One day the boys were playing Cowboys and Indians. I called them together. We sat on the floor in a circle and I told them a story: "Let's make believe you are a daddy with children and a wife. You've built a house to live in. Then some men come with guns and try to take your house away and hurt your family. What would you do?"

"We would fight them. We would shoot them."
And I said, "That's exactly what the Indians did."
They never played Cowboys and Indians again.

During the time between Lincoln's and Washington's birthdays, long before there was such a thing as Black History Month, I taught the children about America. I told them that although we were all Americans, all our families came from other countries. I invited them to bring in something from their family's country of origin. I taught them songs in German, Russian, French and Yiddish; they brought recipes, food and sayings in other languages. They learned that although we were all different, we were really all the same.

For me, teaching meant nurturing children's creativity, enabling them to grow to their full potential. I loved teaching. I was pouring my love out to other people's children all the while yearning to have children of my own.

5
A Tale About a Fairy Tale

Now, about that Nigerian prince and his invitation for me to teach in his country.

I jumped at the offer and said yes. I was a naïve 22-year-old girl from Brooklyn who was already bitten by the travel bug and wanted to change the world. Not only would it be exciting to go to Africa to teach as a guest of a prince, but to be able to live with people in an exotic part of the world would be a dream come true. I was going to be Margaret Mead, the famous anthropologist!

But life had other plans. There is a Yiddish expression: *Der Mensch tracht und Gott lacht* (Man plans and God laughs).

By this time I felt Phil was not going to ask me to marry him, and I couldn't stay in the relationship any longer. I waited five long years and was finally, reluctantly, deciding to break it off. Although I loved him as only a young girl could love a first love, I knew I had to end it if I ever wanted to get married.

During these five years of courtship, Phil and I decided not to go steady but to see other people. I went out with lots and lots of boys but never found anyone else I was interested in, until I met Henry. He was an artist who worked in an ad agency and painted nights and on weekends.

He was attractive, intelligent, interesting and kind. I liked him a lot. Normally, before I would accept a date for a Saturday night with another boy, I would wait until Thursday to respond to see if Phil would ask me. This time, although it was only October, when Henry asked me out for New Year's Eve, I accepted without giving a thought to plans with Phil. He was really on the way out.

Phil sensed something different about me and a few nights later he parked his car in front of my apartment building. He saw me go into the building with Henry, saw the lights go on and off in my apartment and saw Henry leave an hour later.

The next day Phil asked me to marry him.

That was Thanksgiving Day, 1950.

We were married Christmas Day, 1950.

Instead of being in Nigeria the following summer as planned, I was in Corning, New York, at the summer stock theater, the wife of the director Phil Goodman.

6
Anticipating the Big Day

T'was the night before Christmas and Evelyn Twersky was getting married—perfectly calm and without the usual case of nerves many brides have. I was calm with no reservations. I had waited for this day for five years, and it had finally come true. I knew it would not be a conventional marriage, but I did think we would live a happy life.

I went in with eyes wide open. I knew my prospective husband was difficult. It took Phil five years and the possibility of losing me to ask me to marry him. He didn't get down on one knee promising to make me happy with unending love and pleading for me to take him as my husband. In fact, he compared the life he offered me to being on a merry-go-round riding a horse that rode up and down, trying to reach the prize—the brass ring.

He wanted to go into the theater rather than into his father's optical business and become an optometrist. When he told his plans to his father, a gambling ex-carnival man, his father said in true carny fashion, "Better you should tell me you were betting on a 100-to-1 shot."

I had no illusions. I knew it was not going to be an easy marriage, but I felt up for the challenge. His first love was the theater, and I was willing to take second place. Although a psychologist assessed him with a character disorder, I was an eternal optimist. I truly believed that with psychoanalysis, love and time, he would mature and we would live happily ever after.

7
The Wedding

Neither Phil nor I were affiliated with a synagogue, but we were able to find a beautiful space for the wedding in a conservative shul on Eastern Parkway in Brooklyn that was available on short notice.

The band Phil had played with during summers in the Borscht Belt (he made $28 a week plus room and board before enlisting in the army in World War II), played at the wedding. Sid Liss, Phil's best friend growing up, was at the piano, Sid Bodsin on clarinet and for old time's sake, Phil sat in and played trumpet for a number or two.

Good music, good food, good friends and the small family we had. It was a good party!

Because we had announced plans to marry on Thanksgiving Day and were married on Christmas Day, some people thought we *had* to get married. No, we wanted, finally, to get married. Since in those days the Board of Education made no provisions for paid days off for joyous occasions, we thought it a great idea to take advantage of the Christmas vacation for our honeymoon.

We spent our honeymoon at the Park Central Hotel on Broadway between 55th & 56th Street, a great location to enjoy the city.

Unlike in the movies, we did not rush into our hotel room, tear off our clothes and make passionate love on the floor. Instead, we got comfortable in the room, laughed at ourselves as we sat in the bed, opening the envelopes we got as presents, and counted the money.

Looking out the window, we saw it had begun to snow. Perfect!

We melted into each other's arms, made love and fell asleep.

We went to the theater, saw *Guys and Dolls* and *Brigadoon,* ate dinner at restaurants like the now defunct Reubens (famous for its cheesecake), walked on Fifth Avenue in the snow delighting in the department store windows, and went to the Museum of Modern Art.

MOMA was showing a re-run of the original *"King Kong"* with Fay Wray. We had seen the movie once before and it was interesting listening to the reaction of the audience—shrieks of surprise and screams of fear. We laughed. Obviously they were seeing the movie for the first time.

In 1950 there was a housing shortage in New York; apartments were extremely hard to come by. Jac Fast, one of Phil's wartime buddies, had a landlord father who owned a building at 9416 34th Road, Jackson Heights, Queens. We lucked out with a three-room, one-bedroom apartment at a rental of $49.10 per month, and Jac as a neighbor on the floor above us.

We spent our honeymoon "doing New York" and furnishing our newly acquired apartment. We went to the Meat Market district on the far West Side of 14th Street where there were modern designer furniture showrooms. We bought a light-green woven hot dog-shaped couch on brass legs. The Pottery Barn was then a hole in the wall in a decrepit warehouse on 11th Avenue selling discounted china, glassware and other housewares. We bought Artzberg white porcelain dishes, stainless steel cutlery, knives, wooden salad bowls and other household items.

We painted the living room walls rusty brown and used lumber and beige bricks to build bookcases. We had drapes made from American Indian patterned fabrics we bought on 14th Street and found a secondhand upright piano. At Macy's we bought a light wood modern dresser, chest and bed, and in the Village we bought a foam rubber mattress, kitchen table and chairs.

It was fun! It was exciting! We were starting a new and what I thought was going to be a long, happy life.

8
The First of Many

In 1954, Phil now a writer/director trying to break into TV, sold his first script to the TV show "*Rocky King Detective*" for $5,000. We were rich! And instead of Phil spending another summer in summer stock, we bought a '54 four-door Ford for $2,000 and off we went on a cross-country trip. We planned to go the southern route to Los Angeles, stopping in Jonesboro, Arkansas to see Phil's cousins, go up the coast to Washington, and take the northern route back, stopping off in Dubuque and Davenport, Iowa to visit cousins of mine.

Before we left New York, our friends Mike and Nancy Galloway, transplanted actors from L.A., who thought it was glamorous to live in an Upper East Side tenement, wanted us to meet Gladys and Murray Stern, New Yorkers who were going on the same trip we were. We never did because we were all too busy preparing for the trip.

At that time, American roads were empty. I had just gotten my driver's license and was practicing on highways with speeds of 70 mph or as fast as conditions would bear.

We were driving along a long, flat, tedious desert road in Arizona going to the north rim of the Grand Canyon. The occasional cars we passed had license plates from all over the country and either had families with young children or elderly couples in them.

I noticed a car in front of us with New York license plates being driven by the male half of a young couple. We caught up with them and honked. They honked back and after about 10 miles, we came to a rest stop and signaled them to pull in. We got out of our cars and said hello. The rarity of seeing fellow New Yorkers in the wilds of Arizona called for a celebration. I looked at their license plate; it was a Brooklyn plate.

"Where in Brooklyn do you live?"

"We don't live in Brooklyn."

"We bought the car there because it was cheaper. We live in Manhattan."

"So do we."

"Where?"

"86th and West End. And you?

"We live on 84th near Lexington."

"We have friends on 84th Street. Would you happen to know the Galloways, Mike and Nancy?"

"Yes, we do."

And then it hit us all at the same moment. We burst out laughing, pointing at each other, shouting incredulously,

"You're the Goodmans!"

"You're the Sterns!"

They were the couple Mike and Nancy wanted us to meet!

Gladys was a dancer performing for children with the Paperbag Players and Murray was a painter. They had even less money than we did, so that when we got to the Grand Canyon and checked into the cabin we had reserved, Murray and Gladys camped out on our floor.

We told them we were setting the alarm to see the sunrise over the Grand Canyon. Murray, tired and mischievous, with a knowing smile said like a true Philistine, "Why? You've see one tree you've seen them all." This became our laugh line from then on.

We traveled together until L.A., where we parted and made plans to see each other again in the fall in New York at the end of our trip. We became good friends.

9
Babies – It's Not All Smooth Sailing

Being an only child with no cousins and no extended family, I kept asking my parents for a baby brother or sister. I always got the same answer, "After the Depression." That never happened. I knew then the only way to make the dream of my family come true was to graduate from college, get married, have children, raise a family of my own and live happily ever after.

After waiting for five years for Phil to ask me to marry him, and three more years into the marriage, I brought up the subject of babies. I told him I thought it was time to start a family. He said, "No, I'm not ready." Although by this time, after teaching for six years and pouring my love into other people's children and yearning to have a little one of my own, I was smart enough to know not to pressure him and to wait until he was ready. Two more years went by and when I brought up the subject, this time more forcefully, he reluctantly said yes. The first time out, I was pregnant.

The Board of Education looked at pregnancy as a contagious disease and forced me to stop teaching immediately, which actually delighted me. I felt every day was a day playing hooky from work.

Everything was fine until I starting staining in my fifth month. The doctor ordered 10 days of bed rest. I felt scared, but optimistic. On the fourth day I was still staining but had no pain. Phil was out shooting a commercial, and I felt I was getting better. While lying in bed reading a book, I suddenly felt a tremendous urge to move my bowels. I went to the bathroom, sat on the toilet seat, pushed hard, and to my horror, out came the fetus. I caught it in my hands and started to bawl. But, being a curious person, I also examined it. It had a penis and big ears, was still attached to the umbilical cord and was moving its legs. I hysterically screamed, "Stop moving, dummy. Don't you know you're dead?"

I wrapped a towel around me and 'it' and limped back into bed. I called Phil who was filming on 55th Street and York Ave. He got home to Jackson Heights, Queens in what seemed to me to be 10 minutes. I could no longer call it a fetus. It was a baby! I had felt movement and life for a few weeks, and after all didn't it have the Goodman family trait of big ears?

We drove to the hospital with the baby still attached to me both by the umbilical cord and my feelings. I was no longer crying but calm and broken-hearted. I wanted this baby with all my being. I was checked into a semi-private room with a sweet Catholic lady, who took out her rosaries and said she would pray for me. I knew she meant well, but my atheist ears didn't want to hear about God at that moment. I asked Phil to arrange a transfer to a private room. We couldn't afford it but my peace of mind was of prime importance.

As soon as we were given medical permission, we tried again. Bingo! I was pregnant again. By this time we had moved to the West Side of Manhattan and found a marvelous obstetrician, Dr. Bob Feldman at Mt. Sinai Hospital, who became a friend.

I was in my third month. Phil and I were at a matinee of the Frank Loesser's Broadway musical *"The Most Happy Fella,"* and during the performance, I felt a wetness between my thighs. I was staining again! Going from happy to sad in a moment, I decided not to tell Phil until the curtain came down. He might as well enjoy the rest of the play.

I miscarried again. Lying in the hospital, trying to console myself, I was reading Herman Wouk's novel *"Marjorie Morningstar,"* when Dr. Bob came into the room. We talked about my having a myomectomy, surgery to remove the tumors that grew during each pregnancy, and was the cause of my miscarrying.

"Evelyn, I thought about you all last night, and I am giving you the advice I would give my sister. Do you have the guts to try again before we do something as drastic as surgery? "

"Yes. When we can start?"

He smiled. "It all depends on whether you have a semi-private or a private room."

We had a private room.

But this time, things didn't go as smoothly as before. I did not get pregnant.

I didn't get pregnant after trying for almost a year. I looked at the pregnant women in the street. I saw the baby carriages with the little ones in them and I ached all over. I yearned to be a mother. "Why me?" Me, who would make such a good mother, who wanted children so desperately and who was a caring nursery/kindergarten teacher, giving my love to other people's children. I thought of the young girls with unwanted pregnancies who had abortions, or unwanted and unloved babies, and newborn babies who got tossed into trash cans. "Why? Why?" The question plagued me. I remember the answer my father gave me when I asked him, "Why?" and he didn't have an answer.

He said, "Because why is a crooked letter."

Why is the question I no longer ask because I've learned the answer: IT JUST IS.

Call it *beshert*, destiny, karma or even chance. Call it what you will, it is what it is. This is the poker hand we are dealt at birth and we have to play it as best we can. The game is called free will.

I was out of the hospital about a week when friends, Roberta and Ed, whom I had introduced, announced they were getting married and were throwing a party to celebrate their engagement.

Among the guests was an actress friend of theirs, Renee Taylor, who had just read for Phil for a commercial a few days before, long before she became well known. He had told me about her. She was wearing a tight sweater at the reading, emphasizing her large breasts and wore the same sweater when she was called back for a second reading. She wore the same sweater to the party and was flirting with Phil. He flirted back. I walked in on them talking together in the bedroom away from the party. It made me feel awful, doubly awful.

Ed and Roberta were married a year later; I still was not pregnant. After the wedding, Phil and I drove to Acadia National Park in Maine for a vacation. He was very cold, withdrawn, wouldn't sleep with me and cut our trip short. I thought this was his way of showing his upset during this difficult time.

Then the sh—t hit the fan. Phil announced he didn't want to have children. I couldn't believe what I heard. What to do? I went to see my Ob-Gyn, Bob, who told me to leave him. Leave him? The thought had never entered my head. How could I? Even if I did leave him, would I find someone else before my biological clock ran out? I was already 29 and in those days, 29 was very old for baby-making. Anyway, was I able to have children? After all, I did have two miscarriages. And, I loved him.

In a fog, I left Bob's office which was next door to the Paris Theater. I walked myself in, still in a daze. The movie playing was *"The Prince and the Pauper"* with Marilyn Monroe and Lawrence Olivier. I wept through the entire film. All I remember of the movie was the tape playing over and over in my head, "Should I or should I not leave him?"

I decided not to leave him. What I didn't know was that Phil was having an affair with a model friend of Roberta and Ed's. Had I known this, I would have thrown him out and been in a much worse emotional state. Who knows what direction my life would have taken? Would I have gotten married? In time to have children? There would have been no Jody, no Nicky. Inconceivable! Luckily I was spared that path.

Now that I decided not to leave, what to do? I did what many women have done throughout history. I tricked him. I lied. I told him I wasn't ovulating when I was.

It was New Year's Eve 1957 at Lee Strasberg's annual party. We were with our close friends Sandy and Steve Scheuer. Also with us were Richard Burton and his first wife, Sybil, Jerry O'Laughlin with Sandy Dennis and Theo Bikel with his guitar. Everybody was with somebody.

We were complaining that if you weren't on Broadway at the moment, you were nobody at this party, as Lee Strasberg, the head of the Actors' Studio, did not acknowledge you. I had just come from a party with friends where I was accepted and felt attractive, rather than being invisible as a non-actress. Marilyn Monroe was hiding in the bedroom, too scared to come out for fear nobody would pay attention to her. Jerry O'Laughlin was complaining that Sandy Dennis would become a star (which she did) and would then dump him (which she did).

Nobody was paying attention to Richard Burton, a not-very-well-known British actor. At midnight, Theo looked up and said loudly to everybody within earshot, "It's midnight. Let's sing *Auld Lange Syne.*" A woman standing near us turned and answered, "But dahling, I'm not a singer."

When we got home, I told Phil I was not ovulating (which I was) and we welcomed in the New Year making love. The next day we went to Chinatown to our favorite restaurant, as was our custom every New Year's Day. We both got the same fortune in our cookies, "You will have a baby girl." Nine months later, to the day, Jody was born.

Not only was she born exactly on time, but I had a marvelous pregnancy. I took courses at the New School in drama and art. I went to art galleries, theater, cooked, and gave many good dinner parties. Sandy was also pregnant and was a great playmate. Phil and I took classes preparing for natural childbirth, something not popular at the time. Most women made appointments with their doctors for delivery of their babies so that they could be anesthetized and out of it, and the doctors could make plans for a golf weekend.

I wanted to be part of what turned out to be one of the four most profound experiences of my life: getting married, receiving spiritual awakening from my Guru and watching my two babies being born. I wanted to see and experience the birth of my baby; to actually feel the experience. Yes, feel. I was taught to focus on the breath between contractions. There were labor pains, or contractions as they were euphemistically called, but the pain was much less than my menstrual cramps and the end results incomparably different. A baby! My baby! It was thrilling watching the head come out, then the rest of her and hear her cry. I had done it! Unbelievable! From my body came a new life and in only one and a half hours. Unfortunately, the hospital did not allow Phil into the delivery room to share this experience.

The nurses washed her and wrapped her in the prettiest pink blanket they could find. They were excited too. Newborns usually don't focus, probably because they are all doped up. The nurses swore her eyes focused directly on them! She was ugly, and I said so. Wrinkled like a prune, she looked like my father-in-law without his cigar. Dr. Bob said, "How do you know what ugly is? You've never seen a newborn before." He was right. The next day she turned beautiful, and I unabashedly said that too. After all, didn't I say she was ugly the day before? I had earned bragging rights.

In the recovery room, I was the only mother sitting up among the unconscious bodies lying there. The doctors came in to take a peek at the mother whom they called "the natural one."

Nursing was another delight and again something not in vogue in 1958. Having Jody at my breast looking up at me, holding on with her tiny hand, suckling, is something I shall never forget. The feeling of love pouring from me to her and back—of being connected, of nourishing this tiny, living being who was completely trusting, dependent on me. This reciprocal love, given as many times a day as needed with no conditions.

After Jody's birth, it was a good time for both Phil and me. I basked in motherhood and wifehood. To my delight, Phil turned

180 degrees and threw himself into the role of fatherhood. Particularly since I was nursing, he didn't have to share the chore of being awakened for the 2:00AM feeding. Being freelance, he was the reliable, caring, built-in babysitter, and I was the envy of the neighborhood.

Phil was in the habit of inviting people for dinner the same day, giving me very little notice. When I was pregnant I managed to pull it off successfully, but now I was nursing a two-month-old baby with no domestic help. This did not make for successful spontaneous dinner parties, no matter how good my intentions.

One day he invited Geraldine Page, who was a friend, and Alan Pakula, who visited The Actors' Studio for the first time. He fortuitously saw scenes from Phil's play about his father and the carnival and was very impressed, as was Lee Strasberg, unlike his usual self. Alan told Phil to get in touch with him when he finished the third act, as he was eager to start his producing career. I understood why Phil invited him to dinner and graciously welcomed him and Geri.

I was a good cook and enjoyed cooking. I usually tried out new recipes on guests with great results; this time the recipe was a huge failure. Jody wanted to nurse while I was serving dinner and I had to excuse myself. Adding to that, I was terribly embarrassed when I realized I did something that I had never done before. I left a dirty cloth diaper in the toilet bowl. The company was good, and it really didn't matter that dinner was a disaster. But for me it did. Although it was perfectly understandable, I felt like a failure as a hostess.

Alan again told Phil how much he liked his play and to contact him when it was finished. Alan went on to become an Oscar-nominated director-producer in Hollywood, making movies like *"Sophie's Choice," "All the President's Men"* and *"To Kill a Mockingbird."* Phil never finished the third act.

Life went along, and it was good. When Jody was two and it came time to start thinking of a sibling, Phil reluctantly allowed himself to be talked into it. Again, I did not conceive immediately, and we tried for a whole year. When I was finally pregnant, I wondered how I would ever have enough time and enough love for two babies, and if I could love the second as much as I loved Jody. It is possible!

I had a normal, uneventful pregnancy and another miraculous natural birth.

Our friend Nick Lothar took care of Jody when Phil drove me to the hospital. I hardly had time to walk through the doors of Mt. Sinai. Phil was shown to the father's waiting room since they still wouldn't allow fathers in the delivery room. After only 45 minutes of my being in labor, Phil was told he had a healthy baby boy. The other fathers, many of whom had been waiting for hours and hours, were jealous. However, they shook his hand with heartfelt congratulations.

Experiencing the birth of a child was just as thrilling the second time around. Not only did I have a healthy baby, but it was a boy! How perfect!

I lay on the table watching him being washed and swaddled and vowed at that time—1962—that this magnificent, precious, new life would not fight or die in a war in Vietnam. I would do everything in my power to end the war. And I did. I had teach-ins in my apartment, signed petitions against the war and marched in the 1967 rally at the United Nations against the war. The local Democratic club I belonged to came out early, loud and clear against the war. Al Lowenstein, the activist anti-war protester, a member of our club who became our Congressman, galvanized college students into the anti-war movement. Tragically, he was shot to death in his New York office.

After Nicky's birth was a happy time. Jody at four was thrilled to have been given the present of the baby she wanted. All her friends had brothers or sisters, and now she had one too. Phil was surprised and marveled again, as he did at Jody's birth, that I was not depressed and how much I enjoyed my role as a mother. I was overjoyed at having the perfect family—a healthy baby boy and a girl four years apart—and looked forward to raising a family, living a family life and enjoying the fruits of my labor (no pun intended). Phil got his first full-time directing job with a film company and was an active member of The Actors' Studio Director's Unit. All seemed to be going well. Or so I thought.

But Phil was not a happy camper. He was worried. When he declared to me, "I cannot be a father to a boy," I thought it strange but dismissed his fears, reassuring him, "Of course you can." I didn't realize at the time he was telling the truth and that he was having the post-partum depression he expected me to have, since his mother had had a post-partum depression after both her pregnancies. In those days, post-partum depressions were not recognized in men.

I had just finished nursing Jody through a bout of measles while dealing with a six-month-old's schedule on my own. Phil was busy working on a film and was not available much of the time. On this particular balmy spring day in April, Phil was home. Jody was in nursery school and Nicky was napping when he took me aside into the kitchen.

"I have something to tell you," he said, as he sat me down at the kitchen table.

"For the first time in my life I'm really involved."

I thought he was talking about his job.

"I met this Jewish woman from South Africa at the film studio and I'm taking her to London. I'll be back in 10 days."

I sat there stunned, hysteria quietly pouring over me. Tears fell from my eyes and I felt like my heart was split open. I heard his words through a fog of pain.

"I'll be coming back via JFK on flight so-and-so. I'll wire you the exact flight and date."

Was he crazy? Did he expect me to pick him up at the airport like a mother would an errant child? What he didn't know was that once he walked out the door I would immediately change the locks to the apartment and our old jalopy and take out the $800—all of the money we had in the world—from our joint checking account.

Heartbroken and almost penniless, I took care of the children as neighbors and friends took care of me. They took turns, never leaving me alone, bringing me dinner along with their love and support. One got me a good therapist at my request. I didn't know how I was going to make it, but somehow I knew I would.

During the summer I was invited to spend the weekend with my friend Carol Holofcener and Charlie Joffe, the man she was seriously involved with, at their rented house in East Hampton. My parents were very glad to take care of the children at their *cuchalane* (bungalow) in the Borsht Belt in the Catskills. But I had to get them there. Because I drove an old jalopy, driving the 600 miles back and forth from New York to the Catskills and the Hamptons was an enormous challenge. I never knew when the car would break down. Even though I was scared, I gritted my teeth and did it. Only after depositing the children with my parents did I breathe normally, then drove the 100 miles back to the city and the 100 miles out to East Hampton.

At brunch on Saturday, Charlie advised me not to take Phil back, "He will only do it again." I heard him, but didn't listen. Charlie was Woody Allen's manager, who at that time was still a stand-up comic performing at The Bitter End in New York. We spent the day at Woody's and Louise Lasser's house, a small rental on the beach. We spent a delightful afternoon swimming and cooking dinner. It was a fun weekend with good food, friends and laughter. I needed it.

On Monday I drove back to the mountains to bring the children home. Another 300 miles. During the summer, the children spent two more weekends with my parents while I went out to East Hampton with my single female friends. Jody went to half-day camp at Rodeph Sholom. I tried my best to make it a good time for us all.

After six months of sleeping on Sandy's couch, Phil asked to come back. I took him back, ignoring Sandy's advice not to. She knew something I didn't. She told me, years later, the only reason he asked to come back was that he had no other place to go. I took him back because I felt the children needed a father, I had no money or family to help me and, God help me, I still loved him. It was also Nicky's first and Jody's fifth birthdays. The Freudian that I was, I believed children should have a mother and father around until they were six.

Everyone makes at least one mistake and deserves a second chance. I thought we had a chance for the marriage to work, even though in my heart I knew the chances were slim. He didn't say he was sorry, he didn't try to make nice, and he didn't talk about it. In fact, we never talked about it; it was as if it had never happened. I thought he would show me he was sorry by his actions. Ha!

Shortly after our reconciliation, after coming home from a location shoot, Phil insisted a little too hard that I not unpack his suitcase. This made me suspicious, and I unpacked it. In it was a letter from South Africa! I then did something I had never done before or since: I read someone else's mail. In it, she quoted Phil referring to me as an old horse being left out to pasture. After my anger and pain subsided, I burst out laughing. What a discovery after having just been told by my gynecologist I was pregnant!

I couldn't believe it! It was too absurd to be true. It couldn't happen, even to Pauline, the heroine of the melodramatic soap operatic serial, *"The Perils of Pauline,"* which was shown every Saturday afternoon at the movies when I was growing up.

There was only one thing to do and that was to get an abortion. There was no place on this earth for a new life in this toxic situation. When I told Phil I was pregnant, he was thrilled at the news.

"I want the baby!" He was excited.

I told him we needed to terminate it.

"Let's have the baby," he said.

I couldn't believe my ears. What an ego, I thought. "No, I am not having this baby." The tone of my voice precluded further discussion. I thought how ironic; for years it was me saying "yes" and him saying "no." There was no doubt in my mind that having this baby would be worst thing that could happen to all of us. And I did not look back.

In the days before Roe v. Wade I learned something new. I always knew unmarried young girls and teenage girls who "got into trouble," were having illegal abortions. But I didn't realize the extent that married women were. Married women were also desperate for abortions, but they had easier access.

Asking one friend in the neighborhood was all it took to find Dr. Purdy, a socialist, in rural Pennsylvania who believed women should have access to safe medical abortions. Since abortion was illegal, the authorities would jail him every now and then to appease the powers that be as they turned their backs on his illegalities. I called him in Ashland. It was a small town that still had an operator connecting individual calls. When asked for Dr. Purdy, the operator immediately told me he was out of commission until the next month. She knew exactly what these calls from all over the country meant. After another phone call to a friend, I found the name of a doctor in Puerto Rico that she personally recommended. Phil and I made immediate plans. My parents came to take care of the children, thinking we were going to Puerto Rico on vacation.

The doctor's office was small, filled with unaccompanied young girls, two couples and Phil and myself. Everyone was quiet and appeared to be sad, certainly thoughtful. The walls were covered with sweet pictures from magazines of mothers and babies happily smiling. Quite a sadistic sight.

As I was on the operating table, the last thing I saw before going under was a doctor whose white gown, open in the front, exposed his hairy chest. Horrified that conditions were not exactly sterile, but too late to do anything except pray and have faith that everything would be okay, I went under. Hardly an appropriate reaction from an atheist.

Afterwards I rested in the hotel room. Instead of keeping me company and comforting me, Phil decided he was going to the casino to gamble. I was hurt but said nothing. What was I to say? Phil may have either had second thoughts or the casino was a dud because he came back in fifteen minutes. The hurt didn't go away.

We spent a few days in Puerto Rico trying to have some fun. We explored San Juan, went to the rainforest and saw an illegal cock fight in a small village before going home, with me hopeful that the baby-making chapter of my life was over.

10
Picking Up The Pieces and Building A Future

It was a beautiful sunny not-too-hot morning in July, and I was fast asleep. Phil was away on location out West shooting an industrial film he had written; I had asked to be taken along but was turned down. The phone rang and woke me with a jolt. It was Kathy, my last summer's mother's helper in Amagansett. She was looking for Shelly, my New York babysitter and mother's helper.

She had called Shelly's home and her mother had told Kathy Shelly was out West and to call me for details. Unwittingly, Kathy was the pawn Shelly's mother used to tell me my 40-year-old husband was having an affair with her 15-year-old daughter. This 15-year-old was no virgin and no innocent—with a mother who encouraged her to go after Phil and all the social status and money that entailed. However, that was no excuse for a 40-year-old man who was supposed to be an adult.

I held myself together, cut Kathy's call short, and hung up in a state of shock. I wanted to scream; I desperately needed to talk to somebody. All my friends were out of town and so I called 911, just to have a live voice at the other end. I said hysterically, "This is not an emergency. I am not going to kill myself. I am not going to do anything violent. I just need to talk to somebody." Through my blabbering and crying I shouted, "I just found out my husband is screwing my 15-year-old babysitter ,and I need to talk to a real live person." With this, the insensitive policeman on the other end said condescendingly, as though talking to a child, "Oh, lady. It's no big deal. Boys will be boys."

I slammed down the receiver and wept uncontrollably. At that moment, I knew my marriage was over. My world was undone. What was I to do? I had two little children to think about, and I wasn't ready to let go. My first reaction was to have him thrown in jail and her into a juvenile detention home.

After all, hadn't he broken the Mann Act, a federal law making it illegal to take a minor across state lines for sexual purposes? I really savored that scenario for a few moments and was very tempted, but quickly dropped the idea. I couldn't do that to my children; they didn't deserve to have a criminal for a father.

I wiped my eyes and began to think. What was the most rational and practical thing to do? Nicky would be six in October. As a student of Freud, I believed children needed that magic number of years of an intact family life to have a chance to grow and blossom into well-balanced human beings. Jody's 10th birthday was in September. Then there was Hanukah and Christmas. I didn't want to spoil their birthday and holiday fun. I could wait until then. It would also give me time to get ready. Although at that moment I knew for certain my marriage was over, I wasn't ready to break it up and let go of my childhood sweetheart, the love of my life.

I remembered the boy I fell in love with—the 21-year-old, five feet eleven-and-a-half inches tall, skinny (128 pounds), pimply-faced (I never was much for Hollywood looks), but a Big Man on the Brooklyn College campus. He was brilliant, spoke fluent French and Spanish, was a talented writer and actor with a great sense of humor. He wrote clever parodies of songs, did Danny Kaye routines, played trumpet and guitar, sang show tunes and improvised on the piano. He was the life of any party. He drew me cartoons and wrote me love letters. He taught me how to laugh and enjoy food. The boy who was told by his psychoanalyst he had character defects, nonetheless had the whole world at his feet. He awakened Sleeping Beauty and was my Prince Charming. Now my dream of Phil becoming the mature man who would be my love forever was shattered.

I was certain he would become another Elia Kazan, the highly successful and well-known film/theater director. And then in our later years, I dreamt he would teach on a college campus and I would teach and head the Child Studies Center. I shuddered at the thought of all the young, nubile girls on campus; my life would have been a perfect hell. That old chestnut came to mind: Be careful what you wish for; you might get it.

It was extremely difficult for me to wrap my head around a world without Phil. My world had unraveled and come to an end. I needed time and decided to wait until the end of the year to confront Phil. But in order for me to maintain my self-respect and be able to live with myself—and Phil—under these conditions, I couldn't let on I knew what he was up to. I had to live a great big hurtful lie and pretend I didn't know. Lying in an empty bed was lonely enough. Worse yet was lying in bed next to someone I still loved and who was now a stranger—a lying, cheating, ugly stranger who betrayed a trust and broke my heart.

The birthday celebrations and holidays were finally over. It was the night of New Year's Day, and we had come home from a party. The children were asleep. I told Phil we had to talk. We went into the living room and sat on opposite ends of the couch. I confronted him, "I know all about you and Shelly." He sat there, without moving a muscle. He didn't deny it.

Other men in this situation might have tried to say something to ease the pain. Not Phil. He had no concern for my feelings. Quite the opposite. He became cold and combative, sounding almost proud of what he was doing. He wanted things the way they were. He didn't want to choose. He told me, "I don't want to leave. You are my family." Again, not his love, not his wife. He behaved as though it were his right to have a mother/wife and a child/mistress. He was laying down the rules. He wanted both.

I tried to hold back my tears; I couldn't. I did hold back my anger and shame. I was ashamed he was my husband. I was ashamed and sorry I had chosen him to be the father of my children. I bit my tongue and didn't call him the degenerate pervert I thought he was. I pulled myself together and said, "You have to choose. Me or her." It couldn't be both. He told me he didn't want to leave. I was his family, but again, not his love, not his wife. He wanted things the way they were; I insisted he decide. He said, "Okay. Give me six weeks to decide." Why he chose six weeks I'll never know, but I agreed.

I also told him no decision on his part would be taken by me as a decision to leave, and March 1st it was. He had no idea that when I said "decide," I had already made up *my* mind. I purposely let him think it was his decision to make. For him to think he had chosen would make it more difficult for him to walk away from his responsibilities to me and the children. I knew I was asking something very difficult of him since making up his mind was the last thing Phil ever wanted to do. He avoided decisions of any kind. Hadn't it taken him five years to ask me to marry him and five more years to reluctantly agree to have children?

This conversation and its awkward silence brought me back to that hurtful time when Nicky was six months old and Jody four and a half, when he sat me down in the kitchen and said the words I shall never forget, "For the first time in my life, I am really involved."

I had sat in shock and pain then, as I did now.

To add to the madness, Phil and I were building a house together in Amagansett! The March 1st deadline slowly rolled around. That morning, I went to the mailbox to find a letter saying Safeway Builders had absconded with our money and that the workmen had put liens on our house!

Instead of going to pieces, I laughed out loud. What could possibly happen next? Again, I felt like the heroine in *"The Perils of Pauline."* "Yes, life is a soap opera and a dirty soap opera at that!" At the mailbox, I made another decision. If I could spend 17 years of my life in this marriage I could spend another six months getting the house built. Phil didn't mention the six-week deadline and neither did I. That could wait.

Before any further construction, we needed to pay off the liens the workmen had put on the house. This meant refinancing the mortgage. In 1966, at my insistence, we had bought land to build a house. Having no money, we paid for it with money from my New York City Teachers' Pension Fund. The only way we could access the money was for me to resign my Early Childhood teacher's license. With trepidations, doubts and trembling hands, I put the letter of resignation in the mailbox. Although Phil promised to pay me back the $5,200, I knew I was making a life-changing decision, and I wasn't sure I was doing the right thing.

The bank refinanced the mortgage. We borrowed $50,000 with a monthly payment of $108.20 (this was 1967). I paid all the liens and went about trying to finish the house. I called a friend who had a house in Amagansett and asked if I could stay with her for a week. I called my mother and asked if she would come and be with the children. With Nicky in nursery school and Jody at Hunter College Elementary School, they would not be free until the beginning of June.

I went to the house to see what was happening. I drove to Nielson's in Southampton, a huge, wonderful place to buy new and used furniture and household goodies. I bought a new double bed for the master bedroom, trundle beds for the children, and four white wooden chests of drawers that had belonged to an elegant hotel, The Montauk Manor, that had gone bust. I hired a mother's helper; no teenager this time! She was a middle-aged woman with a good disposition and a car, and could help me with the shopping, cooking and driving the children to the beach.

We went out to Amagansett on free weekends. Time was a blur and finally it was June. The children and I and the mother's helper moved into the house. It had a roof and the rooms were framed. That was all! The kitchen consisted of a makeshift sink, a two-burner Coleman stove and a fridge. It was like camping indoors. Gene, the original carpenter and electrician, remained on the job; I still needed to find a painter.

Building was booming in Amagansett and East Hampton. Houses were going up all over the beach and workmen were working two and three jobs at a time. It was a job frenzy. I scoured the beach and talked to workmen with little five-year-old Nicky tagging along. Safeway Builders and the owner Mr. Nussbaum had a good reputation among the workmen. Although he had stolen my money, they didn't want to speak against him. That was not my intention. I told them all I wanted to do was to get the house finished by August 1st, so that I could rent it and try to recoup some of my money. I'd leave finding him and punishing him to others. The men appreciated my attitude, and I think that was why they were willing to go out of their way to help me. When I finally did find a painter, Nicky said, "Don't worry, Mommy. Mike said he would help a damsel in distress."

Gene turned out to be unreliable. He would say he would be at my house at 8:00 AM and wouldn't show up until 1:00 or 2:00 PM. Or, if he did show up at all, he'd leave at 2:00 and Nicky would call out, "Mommy, Gene's gone." We would go to the beach looking for him. It got so bad I began calling him at home at 5:00 AM to remind him to keep his appointments with me. Or, he would come, spend an hour or two and disappear for the day. Finally, I promised him a big bonus if he finished on time.

Through all this, I would call Phil at 4:00 AM in New York. The phone would ring, but there would be no answer. He wasn't home. On the weekend, he would come Saturday morning and leave Saturday night. The children still knew nothing. One Saturday night Phil missed the last Hampton Jitney back to New York. By this time, I wanted him back on that bus as badly as he did. We all jumped into the car and Phil drove like a crazy man to catch the bus in Southampton. Since we didn't have to make local stops, we got to the Southampton bus stop just in time to put Phil on the bus. On the way home, I stopped at the Bridgehampton Candy Kitchen to treat us to our favorite homemade ice cream. I tried to make it fun for them; it wasn't easy. Jody, Nicky and I were all avid big time puzzle-doers. We did the huge 500-piece puzzles. This was one of the rainiest summers I can remember. I know because we finished four puzzles.

We were doing an intricate puzzle of a flower garden and sky at the game table set up near the sliding doors that led to the patio in the back of the house. Without curtains, we could see the night and hear the rain which seemed to me to be forever. The fire was crackling in the huge floor-to-ceiling used-brick fireplace. The smell and sound of the fire and the rain were mesmerizing. My mind wandered; I thought about the hand life had dealt me. If anyone had told me it would wind up looking like this, I would have told them they were crazy.

I thought back to two summers ago at our rented beach house. It was also a raw night. Phil was playing his guitar. We were all lying on the floor, curled up in each other in semi-darkness, the room lit with the light of the fireplace. Phil was singing a folk song. Then he made us laugh with a silly song he made up and we joined in with gibberish of our own.

That summer we had a mother's helper whose father owned a boat in Montauk. On one of her days off she went fishing for tuna with her dad and came back with a fish large enough to feed 10. I quickly called three couples we knew and told them to bring salad and corn. Phil cleaned the fish and made a marinade. I was his sous chef; I was a good cook, but he was a great one. The tuna was broiled and we had a delicious spontaneous dinner party. I loved the time we spent together in the kitchen. It was there we taught two children how to love cooking.

That same summer we swam in the bay at Louse Point and went seining for food for our saltwater aquarium. We never fed our creatures store-bought food. Instead, we bought a five-foot seining net and caught all our own specimens. We had small stripers, snails, hermit crabs, crabs and shiners, their food of choice, which were eaten quickly. We had a large resident crab that had buried itself in the sand in a corner at the bottom of the tank. Only one claw showed.

It would lie in wait for anything that came its way. We once caught a needlefish and dropped it in. The crab snatched it and did away with it as we watched, our eyes glued to the tank. Feeding time was a frenzy and it was not only exciting but taught us about the natural order of the food chain.

Seining is a two-person operation done at the water's edge. Each person holds the pole at either end of the net and together dredge the bottom of the bay with their feet. We got all sorts of unexpected treasures, like that hard-to-find needlefish. The Amagansett haul-seining fishermen fished the same way except, instead of their feet, they used boats and winches to pull in their 50-foot-long nets. The children and I spent many a late afternoon at the ocean watching them fish the same way they had done for hundreds of years.

This particular day, Phil was driving us home very carefully from the beach with our two buckets filled with water and our catch of the day. In spite of his care, he hit a big bump and the water in the buckets shot into the air like geysers. We got all our specimens back into the buckets, we thought, until the next day when we returned to the car. The stench told us one of our specimens had escaped and was still somewhere out of sight.

Another day we went to Southampton to gather mussels, which was another fun, family activity. Since mussels cling to the edge of rocks in shallow water, the whole family could jump in and harvest them. Cooking mussels is no fun. It's a chore because of all the hair attached to the mussels that must be thoroughly removed. We brought home a large quantity, and I spent hours cleaning and washing them. Phil cooked them with onion, garlic, butter and wine. Garlic bread, salad, and wine were part of the meal, which the four of us enjoyed on the patio. Jody liked mussels; Nicky didn't. They ate the bread dunked in the sauce and had seltzer instead of wine.

These were fun times. Now he was stealing the fun from us and giving it to someone else. It made me sad and very angry. My thoughts drifted back into the room. I found an important piece of the flower we were looking for. I fitted it in, and another puzzle was on its way to completion.

It rained on and off for days. It was still raining when the floors were ready to be gym-sealed, and we had to move out. Luckily, we were able to stay at a friend's house. The overnight turned into three because the floors didn't dry due to the rain.

Jody and I loved to go to yard sales and thrift shops. We found an old claw-footed, round wooden dining table and ice cream parlor chairs for the dining room and a rocker for the living room. We drove to Bloomingdale's outlet store and bought a beautiful new grey, black and white tweed six-foot sofa. The side chairs were from more yard sales.

During all this, I still needed a tenant willing to rent an unfinished house. When the agent brought prospective tenants, I would point to each space and say, "This will be the living room, this will be the master bedroom, etc." After only a few days on the market, the house was rented for $2,500 from August 1st to September 10th by a young couple. Now I had a real deadline to meet and had to make good on my promise.

With the rental money, Jody and I went shopping Mid-Island to a department store that catered to Mr. and Mrs. Average Person. Something unique and wonderful happened to me there. For the first and only time in my life, I was able to shop and buy what I liked without looking at the price tag. We bought bedspreads, scatter rugs, linens, towels and throw pillows as they took our fancy. It was fun, and the price turned out to be exactly right. One Saturday afternoon, Phil and I and the children went to Spitz's appliance store in Sag Harbor and bought appliances and cabinets for the kitchen.

In the middle of July, Jody went to sleepaway camp in Connecticut. It was a day trip, and I made it a holiday. We took the Greenport car ferry, crossed Long Island Sound to New London and from there drove to camp. The children still didn't know that anything was wrong between Phil and me; we put on another good act. The day was sunny and being on the water renewed my strength.

I knew the children and I were living in the house without a Certificate of Occupancy. One day a man knocked on my door from the Housing Department and told me I had to vacate because I was living there illegally. I burst into tears and cried, "Safeway Builders ran away with my money. I need to finish building the house and the children and I have no place else to live while I am doing it. I have no money to rent a house." I guess he took pity on me. He calmed me down and said, "Okay, lady. I'll make an exception. You can stay."

One three-day period worked like magic. The sub-flooring in the kitchen was finished. The linoleum was put on the next day and the cabinets arrived on time. Even though the cabinets were too big and had to be sent back to be re-fitted, they were fixed and installed the next day. The appliances were delivered and the kitchen was done. I was making a bedspread out of a sheet, sewing curtains for the bedrooms and making pull-up shades for the dining room. I plopped my sewing machine down in the middle of the living room and began working. This way, I had a better chance of keeping Gene around and seeing that the painter didn't leave. At the end of the day, at 4:00 PM, I broke out the beer. Not before.

By now it was July 29th, and I still needed more time. To top things off, my cat got sick. I took her to the vet who, luckily for me, said she had to be hospitalized. I was much relieved since I couldn't have taken care of her at home. I arranged for Nicky to have a three-day sleepover with his close friend Tony in Sag Harbor. Without the cat, or Nicky or Jody, I was free to focus exclusively on finishing the house.

On the morning of August 1st, I got a call from the tenants. They were delayed and wouldn't arrive until 6:00 PM. Was that okay? It sure was. I was delighted to be given extra time to be able to put the finishing touches to the house. I planted geraniums in the big barrels on the front lawn and back patio. I put impatiens at the front door and entrance walkway. I watered my precious cherry tree, which was thriving on the front lawn I had so lovingly cared for. I finished the shades and hung them on the two five-foot windows in the dining room. I ran to the hardware store and bought hangers for the closets and the window pole for the high living room windows. If you are of a certain age, you will remember the window poles from elementary school. If you were a good student, you could be chosen window monitor and have the honor of opening and closing the windows for a week.

I went outdoors and looked around the house. I smiled. It was beautiful! It was picture perfect! It was finished! I had pulled it off! With whips and telephones, I had done it! I was happy but I was also sad. I was reluctant to turn the house over to the tenants. I wanted to enjoy it with my family—my intact family.

I took a deep breath. It was 4:00 PM. I felt I could give myself a treat and walked to Martell's for a hamburger and coffee. Martell's was just an ordinary restaurant during the day. But at night it turned into the Amagansett mad, swinging singles scene. I then walked along tree-lined Atlantic Avenue to the beach and lay on the sand looking up at the sky, soaking in the warmth of the sunshine. Lying there all alone, staring up into the beautiful blue cloudless sky, I knew that no matter what insanity was out there in the world, I had to leave my marriage. I thought about the little girl from Brownsville who slept on a cot in the kitchen, who now built a four-bedroom house in Amagansett! I knew I could do anything—even enter the uncivilized, lonely singles world.

But before doing that, I made another decision. Instead of wallowing in sadness and loneliness for the rest of the summer, I was going to pay the bills and use the remainder of the rental money to take me and the children on a six-week adventure to Europe!

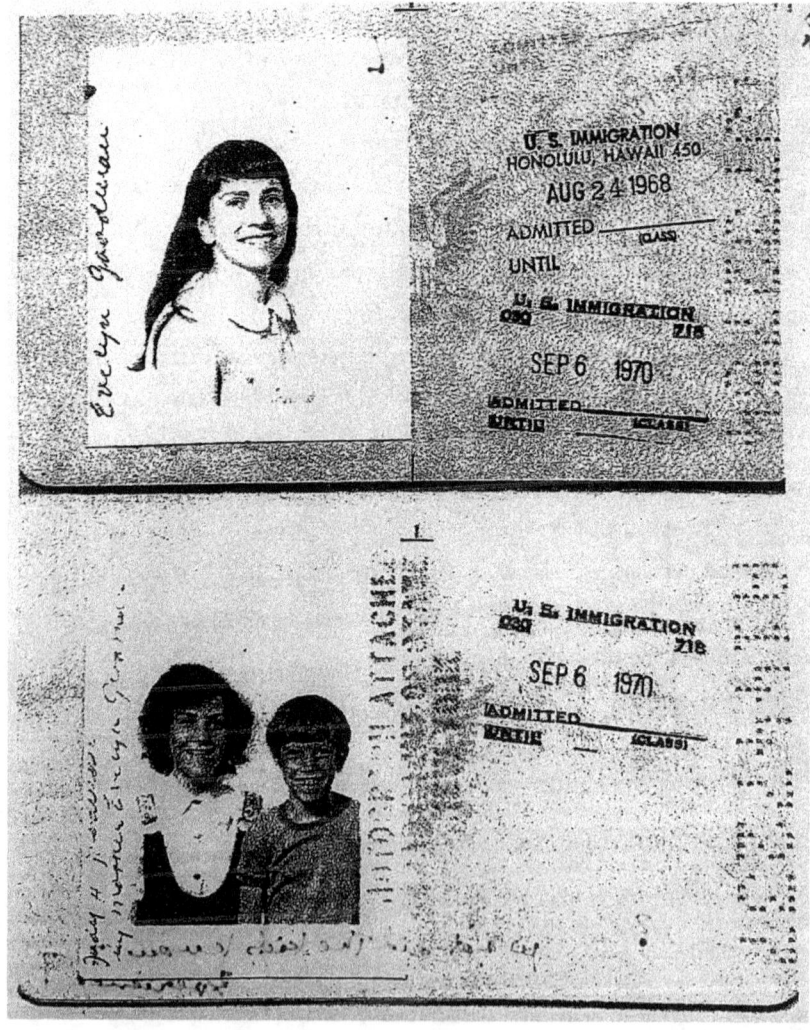

11
Europe Here We Come

My close friend, Ruth Morley was a well-known costume designer who went on to make movies like "*Annie Hall*" and "*Tootsie*," was asked by Frank Perry, director of "*David and Lisa*" fame, to do the costumes for a movie he was shooting in Spain. Ruth accepted despite her deathly fear of flying.

She would take her six- and eight-year-old children with her and asked me if I wanted to join her and bring Jody and Nicky. Without hesitation, I said yes. Watching a film being shot was certainly better than watching the intact families on the Amagansett beach having fun with their husbands and fathers, while I sat there with a broken heart. I knew that refinancing the mortgage, finishing the house and renting it for August and part of September, would pay for the workmen, the house bills and the cost of the trip. The children were good friends, and I could help Ruth with their care.

To tackle her fear of flying, we decided to go to La Guardia airport for a trial run on the Boston-New York shuttle. As we started walking toward the plane, Ruth became more and more agitated. We got as far as the entrance to the plane, where Ruth turned white and literally froze; she could not move. So much for a transatlantic flight; Ruth cancelled the film offer.

I decided to go anyway, traveling on my own for the first time overseas with two small children. People said I was crazy but I looked forward to it as an adventure. We were going to have fun and escape from our pain.

I set about planning an itinerary, making hotel reservations with long-distance phone calls and writing letters (and anything else we did in 1970, the olden days before email and smart phones), bought travelers checks, plane tickets, and enough Spanish pesetas for the ride from the airport to Madrid.

The only food allowance I made for the children was packing a few cans of tuna and a jar of peanut butter, familiar food to help them adapt to Spanish food. But these were cosmopolitan New York kids who had eaten *arroz con pollo* at home and in Spanish restaurants and were able to eat Chinese food with chopsticks. I did, however, pack a thermometer and cough medicine, along with the usual first aid equipment and asked the pediatrician for antibiotics, just in case. I was armed with my broken Spanish, a Spanish-English dictionary, a guide book, and my sense of adventure. Nicky had a small suitcase, Jody a medium one, and I a large one, like in the story of *"The Three Bears."*

We were off to the wonderful World of Oz—Europe.

It just so happened that we were on Iberia Airlines' first 747 flight. I wouldn't have chosen to be among their first passengers, but there we were. Before I could start thinking, "Wouldn't it be better if Phil were here; he speaks perfect Spanish," an interesting thing happened. On the plane, a flight attendant began flirting with Nicky, age seven! My thought instead was, "Thank God Phil isn't here." He would've been flirting with this woman, and I would've felt like *mierda*.

Nicky was busy building a plane. With pen and a large piece of paper he drew a plane and was figuring out how many nails he would need to build a 747. The flight attendant surprised us all by asking Jody and Nicky if they wanted to go into the cockpit and meet the pilot. Nicky said "Yes" immediately; Jody shyly refused. She told me many years later she was sorry she said "No" but was too embarrassed to say she had changed her mind. The pilot gave Nicky a good deal of time, and he came out of the cockpit a happy camper.

At mealtime I learned my first new Spanish word that would come in very handy—*mantequilla*. The butter was wrapped in paper that read *mantequilla*. Everything in Spain was doused in olive oil, not my favorite food. *Mantequilla* was more to my taste.

As we were leaving the airport I asked a man where the taxi stand was. That was when I learned some other Spanish words, *Abajo, cinco minutos, abajo*. (Down the road a piece. Five minutes.) After walking about 10 minutes, I asked again and got the same answer, *abajo*. It was like *mañana* (some time, some place in the future.) The children learned their first Spanish word, *helado*. There was an ice cream stand just outside the airport and I bought them each a huge *helado*.

Just before school ended, Jody's sixth grade class had learned about the paintings in the Caves of Altamira, and I immediately put them on our itinerary. I booked a room at the Gil Blas, a parador in Santillana del Mar where the caves are located. Paradors are government-run and sponsored hotels, often converted from historic mansions, castles, or monasteries. In the hallways of our parador were suits of armor worn by knights of old like the ones the children had seen in the Metropolitan Museum. We were surrounded by a sweet aroma that greeted us as we entered the hotel's flower-filled courtyard. Before we went up to our room, Jody and I played *toro* (bull) with Nicky to tire him out. First he was the bull and Jody the bullfighter; then they changed places. I shouted *ole* and *torero*! We all had a fun time.

I thought things were going well until we prepared for bed. Nicky had a folding bed; Jody and I had three-quarter beds. Instead of getting into his bed, Nicky began to cry, "I want to go home. Take me home." He went from my bed to Jody's bed, back and forth, but neither of us could console him. This went on all night; he cried as if his little heart would break. I didn't know what he expected or what upset him: maybe the knights in armor, maybe the unfamiliar, maybe missing his father, maybe all of the above.

He finally fell asleep, woke up the next morning smiling and said, "I'm glad you didn't listen to me and take me home." From then on he was fine.

After breakfast, we went to see the caves. The walls, instead of being flat, as I expected, were curved. These curves were used to draw the contours of bison and horses painted in vivid reds and blacks, giving them a three-dimensional quality. They looked as if they were going to jump off the wall and smash into us. Their breathtaking strength and power fascinated me. Like so many things I have seen since, I felt lucky to have seen these caves at that time. Due to the moisture in people's breath, the paint had begun chipping off, and the paintings became threatened. The caves are now no longer open to visitors.

In putting together an itinerary, I included both the children's interests and mine: museums, parks, swimming, bullfights, flamenco dancing, boat rides and good food. The caves were the first place we visited in Spain so that Jody could experience something she had just learned about in school and could share her new-found knowledge with us, making her feel more at home.

On the train from the caves to Madrid, the people were warm and friendly, and everywhere we went a hand seemed to appear out of nowhere to help with the luggage or find us a seat. We arrived in Madrid and settled into our hotel for a four-day stay.

Fortunately, because my children were taken to art galleries and museums from a very early age, they enjoyed museums. El Prado, the National Museum of Spain, was my first stop. After getting our fill of marvelous paintings of Velazquez, El Greco, and Goya's cartoons, the full-size color drawings that he created for tapestries that children so enjoy, we relaxed on the grass outside the museum and had a picnic lunch. It was then that Jody felt sick. We went back to the hotel, and I used my just-in-case thermometer for the first time. She had a 100 temperature, went to bed with two aspirin and was better the next morning. That day we went to the bullfights.

The Bullfight

Although bullfighting makes a spectacle out of the cruel killing of an animal, it is a ritualistic sport and is part of the Spanish culture and identity. Being in Spain, the children and I were excitedly looking forward to watching a bullfight.

As we approached the red brick, tile and ornately decorated ironwork building, La Plaza de Toros, the most important bullring in Spain, featuring the best bullfighters facing the best bulls, we were caught up in the excitement of the quick-moving throngs of people, the noise, the flags flying, the banners waving and the music.

It was a beautiful, sunny, not-too-hot day. Our seats were halfway up the arena, but our view was good. La Plaza was filled with 24,000 shouting, noisy, passionate, happy fans waiting for the spectacle to begin. It felt like anticipating the beginning of a baseball game, only much more thrilling.

Before entering the ring, the bullfighters prayed at a little chapel near the Grande Porta. *La corrida* (the fight) began with a parade of all the bullfighters dressed in their *traje de luces* (suits of light). They looked magnificent!

Then the trumpets sounded and the Gates of Fear opened. The leading player, El Toro, a ton of angry bull, was let loose and thundered into the ring. It was an awesome sight.

La corrida is divided into three parts. The first part, *la capa* (the cape) began. The bullfighter tested the bull, making passes with his cape to get acquainted with the animal. My stomach began to knot up with each pass; I feared for the bullfighter.

Then came the second part, *tercio de varas* (sticks) with the lance-carrying *picadores* on horseback who weaken the bull by jabbing him in the shoulders. They were followed by *banderilleros*, who punctured the bull with colored darts.

My heart thumped the entire time, worrying that at any moment the bullfighter would be gored to death. Every pass he made tied another knot in my stomach. The danger was palpable, and I was on the edge of my seat. My emotions were with the bullfighter, not the bull!

I was fascinated by the movements of the bullfighter, as graceful as one of the most accomplished flamenco or classical ballet dancers. I was hypnotized watching his skillful elegance as he proudly teased, prodded, tempted, and challenged the bull. It was a performance of perfection.

The fans shouted *ole* and *torero* if they liked the performance; and hand-clapping and whistling if what they perceived was incompetence or cowardice.

The last part, *tercero de muleta*, was between the matador and the bull. He used a small red cape as a lure and wrapped himself around the cape in different passes. After a number of passes prodding and tempting the bull, the time came for the moment of truth — killing the bull. He did, with one thrust and the arena erupted in wild cheers.

The bullfighter was awarded the greatest honor — *las orejas* (ears) of the bull — and was paraded through the Grande Porta by jubilant fans.

When *la corrida* was over, my stomach was still churning, and it was hard for me to calm down. Nicky loved it and wanted me to take him down into the bullring. We walked down and he stood in the blood-stained sand. That is where my innocent-looking Nicky wanted his picture taken.

He asked me to take him to another bullfight soon and I promised I would if the opportunity presented itself. Jody, on the other hand, was revolted and emphatically said, "Not me. It's barbaric! I'm disgusted! If you take him, I'll stay in the hotel." We never did get to go to another bullfight.

Madrid

I felt very uncomfortable being in Franco's Spain, and would never have chosen to visit a dictatorship had the travel plans not originated with Ruth's movie shoot in Spain. Franco was the dictator who slaughtered his own people in the Spanish Civil War, flexed his muscles by invading Ethiopia in the 1930s, toppling Haile Selassie, its king, and was on the side of Hitler and Mussolini in World War II.

He ruthlessly called in the German Luftwaffe to bomb and destroy the Basque town of Guernica, the subject of Picasso's painting of the same name, which hung on loan in The Museum of Modern Art in New York. The Spanish Civil War, which lasted almost three years and claimed one million lives, was considered to be the dress rehearsal for World War II.

The Spanish people were finally free in 1975, when Franco died of natural causes and the Guernica painting was returned to Spain shortly thereafter.

Fearful that our hotel room might have been bugged, I told the children about Franco sitting outdoors on the grass in the Parque del Retiro. I couldn't be too careful; we were in a country that was a dictatorship, after all.

The 346-acre park was once a playground for the king; now it was a playground for much of Madrid. It was *our* playground as well. We took long, leisurely walks through rose gardens, seeing artists paint and listening to street musicians. We watched the rowboats on the lake. All we could do was watch, since I couldn't row and we didn't have a man to row us around. We picnicked and relaxed on the grass; the children played catch with a ball I had thrown into my suitcase at the last minute.

Sunday was flea market day and El Rostro (Thieves Market) was the biggest and the best. Jody and I loved markets. From the time she was little, Jody had been going to yard sales with me in East Hampton and thrift shops in New York. Nicky enjoyed the bustle and the noise. The market had lots of junk interspersed with antiques and everything in between. I bought beautiful earrings and bracelets for Jody and me and a toy sword for Nicky.

It was hot in Spain in the summer, and the Spanish still practiced the civilized custom of siesta. When Madrid awoke from siesta time, it awoke with a fury. The entire city seemed to be shopping and it felt like a huge outdoor Zabar's, the famous bazaar-like store in New York. Not only were exotic foods for sale, but clothing, home furnishings, bric-a-brac and anything else you could think of. It was a bustling bazaar and the Plaza Mayor was the place to be. I bought some goodies to nosh on to hold us until late dinner, another Spanish custom.

The children were my passport through the streets of Madrid at night. Without them, I would not have been safe walking alone. Men were gathered in groups on the street, making guttural sounds and vulgar, lascivious remarks, which I pretended not to understand. It seemed that women walking unescorted at night were taken for hookers. Obviously, walking with children made it clear I wasn't a hooker, but that didn't stop them. The behavior of the men was ugly.

Even at her young age, Jody sensed the animal quality of their actions, felt uncomfortable and realized something was wrong. "Mommy, the men sound awful. What are they saying?" "I don't understand them," I told her. "Just ignore them and don't turn around."

The children were not able to wait to eat dinner at 9:00 PM, the usual time restaurants began serving in Madrid. But some owners were kind enough to serve us earlier. We went to the Restaurante Botin, made famous by Ernest Hemingway. It had a huge wood-fired brick oven, and we were fascinated watching the three cooks and the streams of racks of suckling pigs being put inside. The roast pork was delicious and so was the *helado* we had for dessert.

Andalusia

From Madrid we took day trips and overnight trips to nearby Andalusia with its beautiful smaller cities of Toledo, Cordova, Grenada and Seville.

Toledo looked as if the painting *"Toledo"* by El Greco had come to life; the sky filled with somber, gray, brooding, dark clouds yet also filled with light. Nature and art were interwoven one with the other. Then the "Master Painter on High" added a bit of reality to the canvas — a small, very old place of worship, a synagogue built pre-1492, situated in a garden. It was divinely beautiful.

Steps led down into a garden to the entrance of the synagogue. I imagined me, a well-dressed Jewish señora of the 15th century on a Shabbat morning slowly walking down the stairs, breathing in the calm, sweet Shabbat air, looking up at the sky on my way to services, sitting in my usual seat in the women's section, praying in Ladino (the everyday language of the Spanish Jews) or in Hebrew.

The synagogue was now a church.

For the sake of convenience, we took my first-ever tour bus to visit Seville, Cordova, and Grenada. One of the popular places to visit in Seville, El Bario de Santa Cruz, once the thriving Jewish quarter, is today one of Seville's most colorful districts. With its winding medieval cobblestone streets and its flower-filled balconies with potted geraniums and creeping bougainvillea and the tangled maze of lanes opening onto a plaza, the area is a delightful place to wander. It was probably a marvelous place to have lived if you were a Jew in Seville in the 15th century!

We saw the stunning Alcazar, the oldest European royal residence still in use by the King and Queen of Spain when in Seville. It was built in the 12th century and was almost entirely rebuilt in 1248. Interestingly, the Alcazar was built for Christian leaders in Moorish style by Moorish artisans. Seeing the magnificent Alcazar, I felt my childhood dream of seeing "Castles in Spain" was beginning to come true.

The cathedral in Seville is the largest Gothic building in the world and the third largest church in Europe with beautiful 15th century stained glass windows. Jody and Nicky were more interested to learn that Columbus was buried there.

The bus stopped for us to take a closer look at the church, and while the guide was talking about the building, I was taking photographs. After what seemed to be only a few moments, I turned around to find the guide and my fellow tourists gone. I couldn't find the bus anywhere. It was Jody who came to the rescue. She reminded me the bus could not fit into the narrow street and was probably outside. Sure enough, it was waiting for us where Jody thought it should be. I knew then I was not a tour person. I needed to look, photograph and enjoy whatever I was looking at in my own time.

On the bus to Cordova, the guide pointed to a castle in the distance and said, "There's a castle, but we have no time to stop to see it." But I wanted to see it; there went my dream of "Castles in Spain." No, I decided, I was definitely not a tour person!

The children and I were eagerly anticipating seeing flamenco dancing. Since flamenco was performed late at night, Jody and Nicky tried unsuccessfully to take naps in order to stay awake for the late night performance. It was midnight before the performance began, and Jody and Nicky were still up.

Men did most of the flamboyant machine gun-like footwork, while women concentrated on the graceful turns and the smooth shuffling step of the *solea* version of the dance. Flamenco guitars were strummed with lightning-fast fingers, with rhythms set by the castanets and the *palmas* (hand clapping) of those who weren't dancing at the moment. The wailing of the singers echoed the Muslim call to prayer; the audience's clapping and whooping and shouting encouraged the dancers.

Flamenco thrives on improvisation; it is a happening. I was mesmerized by the graceful, sensual, bullfighter-like movements of the male dancers, the spirited music and the fervor of the drama. I was enchanted; the children were not. They were fast asleep, one in each of my arms during the entire performance. It was a good try!

Cordova is a medieval walled city. It too had an old Jewish area known as the Juderia with one of the three oldest remaining pre-Inquisition synagogues in Spain built in 1315. After the Inquisition in 1492, the synagogue was first converted into a hospital, then in 1588 into a Catholic chapel.

In every city we visited we saw remnants of Jewish life, and I wondered what impact this had on the children. Did they ask themselves, "What happened to the Jews that lived here?" Jews seemed to live throughout Spain, albeit in separate neighborhoods. Did they leave the country, did they convert, were they expelled? Did they just disappear, vanish, evaporate?

Walking through the crooked, narrow streets we came upon an abandoned statue stuck in a corner. To my surprise, it was of Maimonides, the great 13th century Jewish philosopher. I told the children Maimonides was Jewish and the physician to the king of Spain, as well as being a great thinker of the time and pointed out that his statue was neglected and ignored.

With that I asked, "What do you think happens to a country that treats people badly because of their religion?" And without thinking, Nicky said, "It goes down." And indeed, Spain did go down after 1492.

I had been waiting to tell the children the back story of the Spanish Inquisition and the destruction of Jewish life in Spain. This seemed to be the right moment. However, I didn't think it wise to go deeply into the horrendous details. I told them that the Jews were persecuted and given the choice of either converting or being expelled from the country. I didn't tell them about how the Jews were publicly tortured, such as in the *auto-da-fé* (the public spectacle of renunciation of their Jewish faith and then being burned to death anyway). Those that did convert, called *conversos* or *marranos* (swine), were not safe even after conversion and were still persecuted or killed.

Before 1492 in Spain, Jews flourished and were prominent under the Moors. They were not only merchants but also doctors and lawyers and some became personal treasurers of the king. They were essential to the functioning of the court and country. It was the Golden Age of Spain and it is said that one out of every five people were Jews, which would explain the many remnants of Jewish life we encountered.

The city of Grenada brought to mind the Alhambra — the greatest of all Moorish palaces and one of Europe's top sites that still conjured up the splendor of the Moorish civilization. The Alhambra, an opulent palace with magnificent rooms, flowering gardens, dancing fountains, was also a fortress that once protected a city of a thousand people. It was a bit of magic.

We went through the beautifully decorated arched rooms out into the gardens and fountains. We saw the long pool with rows of water jets making graceful arches above it and a water staircase with water gently flowing down to the next pool. We were enjoying the beauty and tranquility of the moment when Jody began to feel queasy.

We sat near the fountains resting on a bench hoping she would feel better. Nicky brought her water from the fountain to cool her brow and soak her feet, making back-and-forth trips using our water bottle. His attentiveness was sweet; he did it with loving care. Now it was Nicky's unspoken turn to console Jody. It was the same tender loving care she gave him on his first distressed night. They were good friends, and it was touching to watch them spontaneously trying to make each other feel better. They truly loved one another, and I fervently hoped this love would remain between them for the rest of their lives.

The water soothed Jody's spirit, but not her stomach. We took a cab back to the fancy hotel we were staying at and to Jody's horror, she threw up on the front steps at the feet of the doorman. Afterwards, the only discomfort she had were feelings of embarrassment. We settled down in the room and things returned to normal. We played some games, counted the number of Spanish words they had learned so far, and even went for a walk around the hotel.

Plans were made for dinner; Jody was up for nothing more than toast and jam and tea. I ordered room service for Nicky who insisted on eating a small dinner with Jody. I had a dinner date; I can't remember how that happened. I told Jody I would cancel my date, but she insisted I go. "We'll read, play cards and watch TV. We're fine. We can always call the front desk if we need anything." She reassured me and again insisted I go.

Although it was fun to get dressed up and feel like an attractive woman for an evening, I went reluctantly. I remember having good food along with pleasant conversation and coming back as quickly as I could, both happy about my children's mature behavior and sad that they were growing up.

The next day after breakfast we made our way back to Madrid to get ready for a stay in La Costa del Sol, the stretch of beach on the blue Mediterranean coast in southern Spain.

La Costa del Sol - The South of Spain

To avoid the Coney Island quality of Torremolinos, I reserved a hotel in the not-so-crowded, charming, upscale, seaside resort of Marbella. I purposely didn't book a hotel with a pool because Jody and I were looking forward to swimming in the blue Mediterranean and eating *sardinas* grilled on the beach. What a sorry letdown. We got to the beach to find huge pipes leading from the many seaside hotels, dumping their raw sewage directly into the Mediterranean. Vendors were selling *sardinas*, but now neither Jody nor I had the stomach for them.

We left the beach and I found a medium-priced hotel with a pool overlooking the sea. People told me, "You Americans are too picky about not polluting and not smoking." I told them we were just a little ahead of the times. In five years they too would want to protect their natural resources and their bodies as much as we did.

We got into our bathing suits and went to the pool. Nicky wanted to learn to dive but didn't want us near him. He had been taught the basics of diving in camp but couldn't actually dive yet. Since he didn't want us near him, we hid in the restaurant at a window where we could see him and be there in a moment if he needed help.

Nicky began practicing how to stand and how to jump. To our amazement, after a few minutes this little seven-year-old dove into the water. He had taught himself to dive! We ran out, cheered him, embraced him, and we all jumped into the pool. It was better than being in the filthy brown Mediterranean. We swam in the pool, but as people who spent years at the beach in Amagansett and who by now had beach in our blood, we didn't desert the Marbella beach just because people abused it. We played on it during the day and beachcombed at sunset looking for sea creatures and their shells. We just shunned swimming in the sea.

As we were walking, I looked at the people lying on the beach, one next to the other, facing the sun. Doused with sun tan lotion, they looked to me like *sardinas* lying together in a huge, open, sandy, oily sardine can.

Breakfast was included in the hotel rate; we would picnic for lunch. I took myself and my scratchy Spanish to the *bodega* (grocery), where I had to elbow my way through the ladies in the store. There was no line waiting your turn. I waved my arms and shouted, "*Soy proxima*" (I am next), loud enough to eventually get waited on.

We always had fruit in our room to snack on and used the bidet in the bathroom to keep the fruit cold. The toy sword I bought Nicky was used as a supplementary knife. The food was good and the children were willing to taste new foods along with the *arroz con pollo* they knew. By this time we were resigned that everything was saturated in olive oil.

Spain lived up to its nickname, "Sunny Spain," and we enjoyed eating meals outdoors. So did the cats. It seemed natural to us that every cat in Spain came to our table; they knew we were cat lovers. They must have spread the word about us in the feline world because every evening there were more cats to feed. They were scrawny and hungry, and we and the cats enjoyed the feeding time. I thought of

Curry, our finicky cat back home and how spoiled she was, turning her nose up even to pieces of cooked shrimp.

It reminded me of an old Jewish custom. Jewish immigrant European, non-American, mothers urging their children to eat—even hand-feeding them—saying, "Eat. Eat. The children in Europe are starving." I would go back home and impatiently and jokingly say to Curry, "Eat. Eat. You rotten cat. The cats in Europe are starving."

On the day before we were to leave Spain for France, we took a bus to the port of Algeciras and from there a hydrofoil to Morocco, my first but not last venture into Africa.

A Bump in the Road

Traveling from country to country was formidable.

While the cab driver drove us to the train station, I told him repeatedly and emphatically we were going to France and with "*Si senora, si senora*," he put our luggage and us on the train, assuring me it was the express train going across the border to France. We were going there to meet Sid, a close family friend who was Phil's best friend growing up. After the break-up of my marriage, Sid remained my friend.

When Sid married Lillienne, a middle-class French Jewish woman from Paris, his lifelong dream came true. He always wanted to live in Paris and now he was, with a wife and their eight-year-old son Michael.

I had made plans to meet them at the border, then we would drive to St. Jean de Luz, a French seaside border town, where he and Lillienne spent vacations. After spending two or three days swimming and relaxing we would drive to Paris, visit the City of Light and spend time together.

The train made three or four local stop,s and I watched the conductor delivering mail and talking leisurely with the station master and people on the platform. At one stop, three young nuns boarded the train; at another, a young family with three children. I enjoyed watching each scene unfold. It was part of the local color and very interesting. But after a while the charm wore off as I realized we were on a slow, local train. The conductor confirmed my fears; we were on the wrong train. Not only did this train not go to the border, but we would have to change trains and train stations in a nearby town at the last stop.

We were tired and getting hungry. Luckily I had packed a lunch of fruit, ham, hard boiled eggs, and cans of Fanta, real orange juice in a can. It was the first time ever I saw something healthy in a beverage can.

Eventually it got dark. We were getting sleepy and cranky. We, the nuns, the family and one other couple were the only people left on the train. I didn't let on to the children my apprehension.

We finally arrived at the last stop. The train pulled into the station and we all got off. One by one, the nuns, the family with children and the couple were picked up. We were deposited on the platform with our luggage without anyone to meet us. There we were, sitting on our luggage in the dark, at a deserted train station in a foreign country! Somehow I had to contact Sid and tell him of our dilemma.

Not only did I have to find a restaurant or store that was open and had a phone, but I had to make myself understood to the proprietors in a language I could hardly speak. Phone calls between two countries were difficult back then in 1970, particularly when one wasn't fluent in either language. I had to let Sid know we weren't meeting him at our pre-arranged time or even our pre-arranged place.

I couldn't drag the children and luggage with me and made the hard decision to leave Jody—a mature 11-year-old but only 11 nonetheless—in charge. Assuring her and Nicky that everything would be okay, I told them not to move and that I would return soon.

It wasn't so soon. The first restaurant I came to after a five-minute walk had no phone. They directed me to another restaurant; it was closed. At an open restaurant nearby, the owner helped me put a call through to Lillienne who said she would try to get hold of Sid. Hopefully, Sid would call her.

It was a nightmare.

After about 20 minutes, which seemed like forever, I came back to the train station in a cab called by the restaurant owner. Jody began crying, "What took you so long?" I almost broke into tears myself as I told her what happened, and said how thankful I was to have such grown-up children.

I told the cab driver to take me to the train station where trains go to France. He smiled, nodded, said "*Segura* (sure) *señora*," and off we went. I looked out the window and immediately saw that we had left town and were on the open road. After about five minutes I realized he was taking us to the border instead of the train station. For a moment I was indignant, thinking he was cheating a tourist, but then I realized that for the extra few pesetas it would cost he was doing me a huge favor, and I relaxed as much as I could under the circumstances.

After a ten-minute ride we arrived at a station that was dark and deserted. There was no station master or passengers to tell me where I was. I didn't allow my feelings of distress to take over and appeared calm to the children. I saw a staircase, which seemed to lead down to the train platform. "Let's explore the station," I said, as I took the children with me down the stairs.

By some miracle there was Sid! He was surprised to see us coming down the stairs from the street. When he didn't see us getting off the previous train coming from Spain, he called Lillienne who gave him my message.

I jumped into Sid's arms and kissed him on both cheeks. I don't think he ever got such warm hugs of welcome in his life!

I was travel weary and overjoyed to be with Sid. The children and I had been in Spain for a month and although we had fun, it was hard work for me struggling with a foreign language I barely knew, making everyday decisions about where to go, what to see, what to eat, and being responsible for two children. I was looking forward to having someone take care of us for a while, and the next few days of swimming and relaxing with friends sounded like heaven.

The next day, while Nicky was playing with his new-found friend, Michael, I took Jody to a long-awaited treat—lunch at a French cafe. Jody loved to eat, had tasted fine food, and by age 11, was a bit of a gourmet. She was eagerly looking forward to delicious French cooking, as was I. We both ordered cheese omelets and croissants. I had a glass of wine and she had a *chocolat aux lait*. We sat in the sunshine, overlooking the sea, chatting and leisurely enjoying the "Frenchness" of it all. I felt as if I was dining with a sophisticated peer. Doing a grown-up thing with Jody was sweet and a little sad. She was turning into a young woman.

One night I convinced Sid, the homebody that he was, to dress up and drive me to Biarritz, one of the well-known gambling destinations in Europe and only a few miles away. I didn't gamble, but I loved being in the casino, watching people playing baccarat and roulette, the games Europeans played. To accommodate the Americans, there was a small craps table.

I again enjoyed being in the role of a grown-up woman, even if just for a few hours. It felt great to be in France. Although the people in Spain were warm and friendly, I wouldn't miss the pushing and shoving I endured in the Spanish *mercados* (markets). I looked forward to eating food cooked in *buerre* (butter), not olive oil. Learning the word *mantequilla* had done me no good at all. I was served olive oil and looked on as strange. Why would anyone prefer butter when there was delicious olive oil to be had?

After three days of rest and recreation with good food, good friends, sunshine, swimming, and speaking English to adults, I was revitalized.

We were off to Paris, the highlight of our trip.

Paris

Since Sid and Lillienne lived in a small house in Montreux, a neighborhood far from the center of Paris, I planned to stay in a nearby hotel. When I entered the hotel and requested a room in my broken French, the man behind the desk was unhelpful. I could tell he understood me perfectly, but instead of being gracious about my mistakes, he handed me a dictionary. It was both unfriendly and insulting.

I didn't take his dictionary; I just walked out. Nicky, not knowing the French reputation for lack of manners, said, "Mommy, that man was rude. In Spain the people were so happy that you tried to speak their language. He was mean."

Out of the mouth of babes. The Spanish may not know how to line up, and may shove a little too much, but they are friendly and warm, not disdainfully cold. Nicky sized up the situation immediately and perfectly and only seven years old.

Sid insisted we stay with him, and I acquiesced. The children would sleep in the garage. Sid sold antiques in Les Halles, the huge market in Paris and used the garage to store his merchandise. It wasn't The Ritz, but it was clean and usable.

That night Jody and I were looking forward to a Parisian treat—dinner at a fine French restaurant. When Sid suggested the local Chinese restaurant, Jody actually burst into tears. I could hardly blame her.

Sleeping in a garage, in a strange place, in a strange country could be scary. Shadows of the furniture and piled-up boxes were not exactly as conducive to sweet dreams as was a comfortable room with recognizable toys and books. Although they were apprehensive, the children didn't complain; they were amazingly good sports.

Lillienne would pack us a lunch every morning and off we went. The first day we joined Sid at his stall in Les Halles. It was like no other! Along with his merchandise comprised of antiques, almost antiques, and made-yesterday antiques, Sid had set up an upright piano. He was a marvelous self-taught musician who could play anything by ear and enjoyed himself with or without customers.

Sid spoke perfect French and passed himself off as a Parisian. When a customer approached, he would speak English with a thick French accent and pretend to understand very little English. Of course, he then had the advantage of listening to the English-speaking tourists discussing the transaction about to take place. We thought it hilarious but kept a straight face.

The next day we went off to explore Paris on our own via the Metro and an occasional taxi. We were very impressed with the metro. We pressed a button showing where we were and another showing our destination and the route would light up. The stations were clean, the trains safe, and the beautifully sculpted, wrought iron art nouveau entranceways, artistic gems. The taxis were like taxis the world over. The taxi driver cheated me, giving me change in worthless old francs when I paid the fare.

The Eiffel Tower was our first destination. We climbed as high as we were allowed, and standing high up in this venerable Paris monument gave us a glorious view of the city. Our next stop was the Tuilleries Gardens, the large park in the center of the city, to find the Punch and Judy marionette show that enchants adults as well as children. After wandering in the park and coming across the display of flowers in the shape of a clock, and enjoying being in the outdoors, we finally found Punch and Judy. I assumed Nicky would love it, but to my surprise, he was spooked again. He was very upset, saw nothing funny about the slapstick humor of the marionettes, and wanted to leave immediately.

We went to the Les Marais and Rue des Rosiers, the Jewish quarter in the third and fourth arrondissements, where we bought sour pickles and knishes. The neighborhood was a polyglot of old-time Jewish residents, young bohemians and new immigrants.

We not only spent time in the market watching Sid sell his wares, but took a boat ride along the Seine and went for a long walk along its banks; visited Notre-Dame and walked along the Champs

Élysées to the Arc de Triomphe. The Musée d'Orsay had a show of Matisse cut-outs, which enchanted the children. Of course, seeing the Mona Lisa at the Louvre was not to be missed.

Climbing the stairs in Montmartre, watching the men wearing berets, carrying long baguettes coming home from work, I caught the excitement of the moment and the city, and felt like a character in that marvelous film about Paris, *"The Red Balloon."* All that was missing was the balloon, and I excitedly shouted out in disbelief, "Hey kids! We're in Paris!" We stopped for snacks at a *patisserie* (bakery) or an outdoor cafe, and had an occasional lunch at a fancy restaurant.

After a day of sightseeing, we went back to Sid and Lillienne's for dinner. He would tell stories, play the piano and entertain us with his impersonations. His best was that of a Jewish Cockney. His accent was impeccable; the combination unimaginably funny. The first three nights were fine. Jody and Nicky had gotten used to their less-than-perfect sleeping arrangements, when on the fourth night Jody woke up in a panic screaming in pain. When we turned on the light, we saw the wasp that had stung her, dead in her bed. We searched for a wasps' nest, but found none in or near the garage. While this may have allayed Jody's fears, I am sure she was not comfortable sleeping there. However, she never complained and made the best of it.

England

When it was time for us to leave Paris for England, Sid spontaneously decided to travel with us and drive us to Lillienne's aunt Eunice in Brighton.

The ferry crossing the English Channel accommodated cars, and while Sid was acclimating himself to the English "driving on the wrong side of the road" by mumbling constantly, "Keep to the left, keep to the left." I was changing money once again, this time from francs to pounds. I explained to the children that although the money looked different from dollars, it was not Monopoly play money like an "ugly American" aboard the ferry had loudly dismissed it.

Aunt Eunice was lovable and a character. She looked, sounded and acted like the British comedienne and film star Hermione Gingold, but without her sense of humor.

After a day spent swimming on the rocky beach, watching the waves crash over the sea wall, and an overnight at aunt Eunice's, we said goodbye and I booked seats on the Brighton Belle, the train to London.

The station was long and so was the train. I put our luggage on a cart and began wheeling it down the platform. It made loud creaks and groans, which turned many heads toward us, much to my embarrassment. I peeked into the windows of each car we passed, looking for coach seats. I said to myself, "This couldn't be for us," as each compartment we passed had a table with a white table cloth, china and silver set up to serve four people. I presumed it was a first class compartment. Amid laughter and self-consciousness, in what seemed like forever, we creaked and squeaked down the entire length of the train to the last car. I realized then that the entire train was set up for elegant tea-time for all the passengers!

We boarded and went into a compartment. I was relieved we were no longer the center of attention of the entire platform. We took off our jackets, sat at the beautifully set table and began to get used to the idea that we were going to be treated to the luxury of tea with the finery of china, crystal and linen.

Soon after the train left the station, a porter came to serve us tea sandwiches, pastries and tea. We were delighted. But the train was no plane. Picking up the cup without spilling it was hard enough; getting it to our mouth without spilling it was next to impossible. The tea jumped up from the cup like a geyser. We giggled, then laughed, then exploded with laughter with each try. Of course the beautiful linen cloth was completely tea-stained. We tried to keep it clean, but that was next to impossible.

The thing I remember most was our uncontrollable laughter and the fun we had managing the unmanageable. In between our peals of laughter was the laughter we heard coming from the neighboring compartment.

When the train reached London and expelled its passengers, euphoria was queen. Everyone was laughing or had a silly grin on his or her face. It was a fun, explosively laughter-filled ride from Brighton to London.

Regrettably, the ride is no more. "The Brighton Belle" no longer exists. But thankfully London does! Three days in London. Hardly enough! And how marvelous to be in a big city where people spoke English!

By the time we left Spain, the children could understand or say about a hundred words (for Jody) and about 50 words (for Nicky) in Spanish. Starting with *helado* and *mantequilla*, they learned *por favor, gracias, buenos dias, adios, muchacho, muchacha, señor, señora, señorita, el gato, el toro, bueno, donde esta, el baño, cuanto, ahora, si* and many other everyday words.

Ditto for France: *bonjour, adieu, merci, s'il vous plait, mademoiselle, madame, garcon, monsieur, oui, ou, combien* and about 30 other words.

But now we were in London where people spoke English. Or did they?

I had reserved a hotel room with twin beds and a cot for Nicky, only to find a baby's crib in our room. That was when we realized there was a third language we had to learn—British-English. The old chestnut that England and America were two countries separated by a common language was alive and well. Keeping an ear out for British-English made our exploring London even more interesting.

Our first stop was Buckingham Palace to see the Changing of the Guard. There was a large crowd of people in front of us making it impossible for Nicky and Jody to see the soldiers marching in front of the palace. They were very disappointed and as we wondered if we should come back another time, a bobby (policeman) accent, "Little boy. Would you like to see the soldiers?" Nicky eagerly said, "Yes" and I thrust the camera into Nicky's hand as he was taken through the crowd to the palace gate. For days afterward, Nicky played "Changing of the Guard" as he stiffly marched, leaning at a 45-degree angle, from place to place.

From there we rode a double-decker bus to get an overview of London, seeing the famous Big Ben, Parliament and Westminster Abbey, the burial place of kings, queens and other notables of English history.

While walking through the Abbey, we happened upon the grave of Benjamin Disraeli. I told the children he was the first Jewish Prime Minister of England and had the honor bestowed upon him of being buried with the monarchs of the country.

I reminded them of the neglected statue of Maimonides in Cordova and told them Maimonides was buried in an obscure place in Tunisia. I pointed out the difference between the present Spanish dictatorship, the cruel Spanish monarchy of 1492 and the present democratic monarchy of England where people were free to practice their religion of choice. We got off the bus at Hyde Park to hear the speakers at Speakers' Corner and enjoyed adding to our list of unintelligible words.

The next day we took a boat ride on the River Thames to see the Tower of London and Tower Bridge and were entertained by buskers (street performers). This brought us to the East End, a poor neighborhood of London, formerly Jewish with remnants of Jewish life. Jews who lived there moved to middle-class neighborhoods as they became affluent, making room for the next wave of immigrants. No forced exit here.

Because the Jewish restaurant I had planned on for dinner had closed for the Sabbath earlier than I anticipated, we couldn't taste English-Jewish cooking. Jewish cuisine is different in every country. We went to a nearby Chinese restaurant; wherever there are Jews, there are Chinese restaurants. The general wisdom is you can get good Chinese food anywhere in the world; England proved to be the exception. It was the worst Chinese food we had ever tasted and we were even charged for tea which is unheard of in New York.

Looking at paintings in the National Gallery, Nicky called out, "Ma." I thought he was calling me, but no, he was very excited as he came upon and recognized, Ma—tisse, cut-outs similar to the ones he saw in Paris.

With the help of unusually good weather we were able to see a great deal of London during our three-day stay. Our list of British-English was getting very long and we would quiz each other at meal times trying to memorize some particularly quaint words.

Among the list were:

Put a sock in it	Shut up
Prat	Idiot
Snogging	Kissing
Dummy	Pacifier
Nappy	Diaper
Blow-off	Fart
Tight as a fish's bum	Cheapskate
Fruit machine	Slot machine
Punter	Customer
Pissed	Drunk
Fringe	Hair bangs
Pear shaped	Gone wrong
Stroppy	Bad-tempered
Take the mickey	Tease

A Traveler's Tale - in British English

We queued up for our luggage to be put in the boot of the petrol-powered coach and headed off to the country on a top-hole dual carriageway. This turned into a road with many roundabouts and sleeping policeman. We passed a queue of lorries on the road and because of the dark, we needed cats' eyes.

We wore our macs over our jumpers, but our gym shoes got wet even though we had our bellies and brollies. We needed to spend a penny, but while looking for a loo, we stopped at a car boot sale. On the coach we played Chinese whispers, noughts and crosses and draughts.

For dinner there was fish-n-chips, goujons with marrow or tappie scones, kippers, and courgettes. There were also faggots or a rasher of bacon. For dessert there were lady fingers or an iced jelly or a digestive.

Drinks were a cuppa or lemonade.

Piccachilly made everything taste better.

Hard cheese was inedible.

Faggots were not allowed on the coach.

Translation:

We lined up for our luggage to be put in the trunk of the gasoline-filled long-distance bus and headed to the country on a first rate divided four-lane highway. This turned into a road with many traffic circles and speed bumps. We passed a line of trucks on the road and because of the dark we needed reflectors.

We wore our raincoats over our sweaters, but our sneakers got wet even though we had boots and umbrellas. We needed to pee, but while looking for a bathroom we stopped at a temporary flea market. On the coach we played telephone, tic-tac-toe and checkers.

For dinner there was fish-n-chips or fresh fish or chicken sticks. There was also sausage or slices of bacon. For dessert there were cookies, popsicles or round graham crackers.

Drinks were a cup of tea or soda.

Relish made everything taste better.

Bad luck was not edible.

Cigarettes were not allowed on the bus.

A Parting Farewell

Your language is wonky but we remained brilliant. Ta ta, you Brits. We moggie-loving Yanks had a jolly good time!

Your language is weird, but we remained cool. Thank you, Brits. We cat-loving Americans had a marvelous time!

Regretfully, it was time to leave London and head for home. Three days was not enough but I knew we would all be back, probably separately, with friends, lovers, spouses or in the case of the children, with children of their own.

Going Home

The trip was a fairy tale come true. It was great being with Jody and Nicky and being the person they just played with, like the babysitter or the older playmate. We were far away from home, in foreign countries, hearing many languages other than English, tasting new delicious exotic foods, not doing homework or chores, having exciting new experiences and getting to know each other and enjoy each others' company without encumbrances. The trip gave us the fortitude to face the reality that we were no longer an intact family and gave me the strength to begin to heal a broken heart.

We got to Heathrow Airport with the equivalent of $50 in my purse, just enough to buy earphones for the movie on the plane and to pay for the cab fare home from the airport. In the cab, the real world, via the radio, came crashing in on us like a hurricane.

The TWA plane that Jody's best friend and her sister were on, going from Israel to New York, was hijacked and the passengers were being held in the desert as hostages. The girls flew El Al every summer to visit their mother, who lived in Tel Aviv. This year, for some reason, they decided they would be safer on TWA. What irony.

Not only did we fear for their lives, but Jody's friend had asthma and we were afraid she would get an attack and not have the medical attention she needed. The hijackers had wired the plane to explode at any moment. After a week of dreadful worry, some of the passengers were released and the girls came home safely. The hijackers eventually blew up the empty plane.

It was a most dramatic and unexpected ending to our most unusual summer.

12
Back Home to the Real World

Home and back to the reality of what lay ahead—no marriage, no money, no job, children who needed extra tender loving care, and me, alone, with a broken heart.

I plunged into starting a new life: unpacking, getting the children ready for school and doing the mundane things of everyday life: crying at times, having fun at times, taking the children on excursions around New York, maneuvering to keep them from learning the truth about their father and their babysitter, trying to put the pieces of my life together again without Phil, while being sad, angry, bitter, lonely and broke.

Instead of going back to teaching and the comfort of a job I did and knew well, I became a TV producer on a show called "All About TV" on the city station Channel 31, hosted by Steve Scheuer, the executive producer. It was the first talk show on TV, before David Susskind and long before Charlie Rose. It sounds like a wonderful job, and it was, except for the fact that due to a lack of funds in the city's budget, the salary was minimal.

For money, I became a substitute teacher and got sporadic, meager child support and alimony from Phil. I rented out the Amagansett house, which paid for itself, sent the children to camp and supplemented my paltry substitute teaching salary enabling me to begin my travels around the world.

13
The Secret Ingredient in the Turkish Delight

In 1973, while volunteering as the Bronx Coordinator for the Al Blumenthal campaign for Mayor of New York City, I met Nan, a fellow volunteer. She had lived in Turkey with her ex-husband, who was stationed there with the American army, and was eager to explore Turkey beyond Istanbul.

She couldn't find anyone to go with her until I jumped at her invitation with an enthusiastic "yes." We made plans to go the following summer while Jody and Nicky were at sleep-away camp. At that time, Turkey was a remote, unsafe, unpopular destination for American tourists, considered especially unsafe for two females traveling alone without male protection.

Living in Turkey, Nan learned some customs that would help keep us, as women alone, safe. One major one was to honor the Turkish age-old custom of dressing properly. This meant having our arms covered and our skirts below our knees. Another was to honor the custom of allowing the man to be in charge and make the decisions. If a bus driver said to sit behind him, you did so because now, in his bus, he was responsible for your safety as you rode with male passengers. (I heard a story of a bus driver who forcibly evicted a male passenger onto a deserted dark road because he had put his hand on a strange woman's lap). A cab driver would physically hand you over to the male concierge of your hotel. You went from male hand to male hand, and you were safe. Nan also knew that if two females walked down the street arm-in-arm, they were recognized to be Turkish women, not tourists, and so were safe.

In any case, lack of safety was not on my mind. Turkey sounded like an exotic and fascinating place to visit and I wanted very much to go. In doing research for the trip, I consulted with my new friend, Gerald Sykes, a professor at the New School. In my new life of separation from Phil, Gerald, whose class I sat in, filled the role of intellectual companion, one of the things I sorely missed. He was a Renaissance man and an inspiration to many artists. He told me about a place in Turkey, Çatal Höyük, an archeological site dated 7,500 B.C.E., considered to be the oldest matriarchal society excavated to date. My fascination with archaeology was awakened, and I had to take Nan to see it.

We took a local bus from the small city of Konya, the land of whirling dervishes and home to Rumi, the great mystic poet of the 13th Century. The bus driver told us to sit in the back, and we, two 1970s American feminists, did as we were told. There were five or six veiled women sitting with their babies and baskets of fruits and vegetables on their laps. We smiled and sat down among them. Our eyes met to say hello. After a few minutes, I asked one woman if I could hold her baby on my lap. She handed me the baby and I felt the deliciousness of a baby in my arms. Nan did the same. The women opened their baskets and gave us fruit. We graciously accepted and spoke to each other with our eyes. They gave us the babies, the fruit, and the pleasure of their company. It was a sweet moment.

The bus let us off at our destination, a small village in the middle of nowhere with unpaved dirt roads, narrow tiny sidewalks, and just a few stores and huts. A cab was waiting at the bus stop and took us to the excavation site. Along the road we saw mounds of earth called tels, (unexcavated former civilizations) waiting to be uncovered and brought to life. The countryside was also dotted with white three-sided huts (much like Jewish *sukkahs*, temporary dwellings), which farmers built in the fields for protection from the elements. No houses, no civilization; just telephone poles.

When we got to the site, we watched the excavation. A large, corpulent archaeologist was so engrossed in his work that he didn't notice his pants were falling down halfway below his rotund belly. I said hello and could tell by his accent he was British. But he was not interested in talking with us; he would rather get back to work. Four or five people were busily digging and sifting what seemed to be to the inexperienced eye, just dirt.

It was hard to imagine that this would become a World Heritage Site attracting many more than two lone tourists. The artifacts, small voluptuous female statues looked surprisingly modern like Henry Moore sculptures; they were displayed in a gem of a museum, an old converted covered bazaar, The Archaeological Museum in Ankara, the capital of Turkey.

After watching the archaeologists work for awhile and feeling very much in the way, we took our waiting cab back to the village, where we could catch the bus back to Konya. We got on the bus and in the few moments it took to take out the fare, Nan realized she had no purse! She had left it in the cab! In it was everything—money, credit cards, traveler's checks (those ancient items), and passport. The bus driver turned the bus around and let us off in the village. Nan, the experienced traveler, had a meltdown. Me, the novice, told her not to worry. We would find her purse.

I walked over to the first man I saw. I knew no Turkish. How to talk? He knew no English—or French—or Spanish. What to do? And then I remembered! Nan had told me that the Turks went to Germany in the summer to work, and in fact we had seen some poignant goodbye scenes at the airport.

Aha! He might know German!

"*Sprechen Sie Deutsch?*"

"*Jawohl,*" he said. And we both smiled.

I knew only a tiny bit of German, but I had grown up in a Yiddish-speaking home! That is, my parents spoke Yiddish to each other and English to me. And so, although I understood Yiddish, I was never able to practice speaking the language. Here was my chance! I began speaking in my *tzebrucheneh* (broken) Yiddish—adding a sprinkling of my German 101—to this Turkish man in nowhere land!

He understood me perfectly! While telling him what happened, the people of the village were gathering around us. We were a rare sight: two women in the wilds of Anatolia, traveling without veils and without a man.

He told us, in German, not to worry. Before he got on his bicycle and started the search for the cab driver, he made sure we were comfortable. People brought us chairs and two boys brought us some chai carried in a big, beautiful carved wooden box that looked like the shoeshine boxes used in train stations in America years ago. We drank the delicious, strong, sweet tea in silence and acknowledged its good taste with a smile.

The women, all veiled, put their faces within an inch of ours, marveling that we were unveiled and traveling alone. They were transfixed; I felt they wanted to touch us to make sure we were real. This feeling went both ways. Looking out at the vast flat countryside, with only one straight road running through it and nothing but white huts sprinkled sparsely on the land, felt timeless. Except for the telephone wires, I could have been living in biblical times.

After about fifteen of the longest minutes I have ever spent, the man came riding around the corner with a big smile on his face, waving at us. On the handlebar of his bicycle was Nan's purse!

"*Danke schön! Danke sehr viel. Danke!!!*"

"*Bitte schön!*"

My *Tzebrucheneh* Yiddish saved the day!

14
Greece—Land of the Gods

After Turkey, Nan and I split. She went on to Cyprus, and I went off to Greece for my three-week adventure alone. Before ever getting there, I had an unexplainable premonition that in going to Greece, the land of inspiring temples born of myths, oracles and magic, I would encounter the Gods.

At this time, I was producing my TV show and very much wanted to get a press pass before I left for Greece. I felt it would be my key to all sorts of interesting places, and as a woman alone, it could be a safe entrée.

I called the Greek Embassy and was told to contact the New York Consulate. There, I spoke to an interesting young man, the head of Public Relations. Although he wanted to help me, he regretfully could not get me a pass in time for my trip. He wished me bon voyage and off I went.

A big city girl in a big city. Athens! What fun! Except that for the first time in my life, I was illiterate! I couldn't read the street signs or the newspaper headlines. The alphabet was different. How strange, and how humbling. Being by myself and not having someone to talk to, I was much more open to speaking to strangers. In one such conversation, sitting with a man at a cafe, I asked something I had been pondering for a long time.

"In America, when something is very difficult and incomprehensible, we say 'It's Greek to me.' What do you say?"

He smiled and replied, "We say, 'It's Japanese to me.'"

During my week in Athens, I went to a concert at the Parthenon, the amphitheater built by the ancient Greeks. The seats were the original rows of ancient stone, with no backrest and as uncomfortable now as they were then. Only two rows in the entire stadium had backrests. Although I was in my early 40s, I had severe back problems and I already needed support for my aching back. I went to the box office to request a seat change and was given one on the opposite side of the amphitheater, far from my original seat. Sitting next to me was a very attractive middle-aged woman.

The night was clear, the sky filled with stars and the music particularly beautiful in these surroundings. Enjoying the ambience and the music didn't stop me from counting the women in the orchestra. It was the 70s after all. When intermission came, I turned to the woman next to me and said, "There are only seven women in the orchestra." She smiled and said, in perfect English, "I counted them too."

We began talking and introduced ourselves. She told me she was divorced and had two sons, one living in the United States.

"Where does he live?" I asked.

"In New York."

"What does he do there?"

"He works for the Greek Consulate."

"Really?"

"Yes, he's the head of Public Relations."

I gasped as I realized that her son was the last person I had spoken to in the U.S. before I left for Greece!

Gerald Sykes had a home in Greece, and I relied on his advice in putting my itinerary together. I asked him what the Athenian equivalent of East Hampton was and he said the island of Hydra. After a week of being by myself, making all necessary arrangements, I wanted some tender loving care and therefore booked a day-long tour to Hydra, with free time on the island. As part of the tour, lunch was served on the boat deck and the passengers, from all different countries, were seated at a long table.

I sat opposite a woman I thought to be Japanese-American. We started talking. She told me she was born in Japan, left for England as a teenager and was now married to a British doctor.

"I've been to Japan."

She smiled.

"It's a beautiful country, and I fell in love with it. When I was there, I told my friend Emi, my traveling companion at the time, 'I must come back. Only next time it will be with a man.' "

She sat up straight and became very interested, "Emi, who?" The woman asked.

"Emi Suwata Kamiya."

She smiled, looked directly at me and announced, "Emi was my best friend! We grew up together in Tokyo. She taught me English."

A big city does not a country make and after a week, I was ready to leave Athens and experience more of Greece. I chose the Peloponnese, a peninsula of about 8,000 square miles, separated from the mainland by the Gulf of Corinth. There was no other way to get there except to take a bus tour, which I did though I was loathe to do it. Driving through the mountains was treacherous, on a road with breathtakingly sharp curves and no railings. Along the road were small white crosses marking the graves of those who hadn't made it.

After seeing Sparta, home of the Olympic games, Mycenae and its temples, Olympia and other great archeological sights, we transferred from the bus to a boat to take us across the Isthmus of Corinth. Getting off the bus, I spotted an elderly gentleman wearing a straw hat, looking very much like Maurice Chevalier in a French movie, sitting at a round white metal cafe table. He looked up and asked in English with a thick Greek accent, "Anybody an American? Anyone speak English?"

I answered, "Me," and walked over to join him. He invited me to sit in the empty ice-cream chair beside him. I thought it would be interesting to talk to him, particularly since we had some time before our ferry arrived. He told me he had lived in the United

States for many years with his wife. He loved America and was very happy until she died two years ago. He was bereft and if it weren't for his two very close friends, who invited him to dinner two or three nights a week, he felt he would have died of a broken heart. His doctor finally suggested that moving back to Greece might be the best option for him. He did, but he missed America very much, as well as those two dear friends who kept him alive.

"Where in the U.S. did you live?"

"In a small town down south."

"Where?"

"In a small town in Arkansas."

"Where?" I persisted.

"Oh, you wouldn't ever have heard of it."

"Try me. I've been to Arkansas. My husband has cousins in Jonesboro."

He excitedly said, "That's where I lived!"

I then asked, "Did you know the Goodmans? Herbert and Joan? He was the manager of the Black and White Department Store."

He jumped up all flushed with disbelief and said, "Herbert and Joan were the friends who saved my life!"

He was moved to tears and wanted to talk more. He invited me to his home and I very much would have liked to accept his invitation, but unfortunately I was on a tour and wasn't free to do so. When the boat arrived, he handed me over to the Captain for safe keeping. He sadly waved his hat; I waved my hand. We reluctantly said goodbye, and the boat sailed away.

Yes, Greece was indeed the land of magic!

Coincidences? I don't believe in coincidences; they are not random happenings. To me, coincidences are a "God nod." It's His/Her way of staying in touch. A Hasidic saying, "God plays "hide and seek," but is afraid no one will look for Him.

"Coincidences" are God's way of saying "Hello. HERE I AM."

15
Keeping My Promise

Time went on: school, extra-curricular activities, sleep-overs, sleep-away camp, play dates with friends, child care, working, trying to keep things together, making life for all of us as fun as possible without an intact family, dating, seeing friends, celebrating the Jewish holidays and keeping my promise to make the children know and love who they are as Jews.

I had sent them to nursery school at Rodeph Sholom Synagogue, a reform shul on the Upper West Side. However, when Jody at age four came home and said she wanted to light candles on Shabbos, I couldn't be a hypocrite. I told her that was for school. And when she asked me one day, "Is there a God?" I didn't say "No." Instead, I told her, "Some people think there is." She was smart enough to figure out I didn't believe.

I had raised an atheist, which would come back to haunt me.

We celebrated all the holidays. We had an annual Hanukah party which the children's friends loved. They played "spin the dreidel" (top) with shiny new copper pennies they could keep, and of course, there was Hanukah *gelt* (chocolate coins) for them to eat. They ate potato *latkes* (pancakes), sang songs and lit the menorah candles. It was great fun. My children got a Hanukah present on each of the eight nights, so much better than the one Christmas present.

I must confess we, like all our Jewish friends on 86th Street, also had a Christmas tree. I was conflicted; I didn't really want a tree but came up with good reasons for having one. My niece Florence, who lived in Levittown, cried every Christmas because she couldn't have a tree. She was told it was because she was Jewish. I didn't want my children to feel less than their non-Jewish friends. And most importantly, since Phil very much wanted a tree, I agreed. Now, with Phil gone, so was the tree.

I didn't call the tree a Hanukah bush. I explained to the children that they went to their friend's birthday parties and celebrated with them even though it wasn't their birthday. In the same way, we were celebrating the birth of Jesus, even though Christmas was not our holiday. Jesus was a great man who also was Jewish.

They baked *hamentashen* (three-cornered cookies) with grandma on Purim and learned the story of Queen Esther and how she saved the Jewish people from the villain Haman and destruction. We went to my parents for minimal Passover seders and had great seders with friends.

When Nicky was eleven-and-a-half, I started thinking about his Bar Mitzvah. Hebrew School and Bar Mitzvah study was a two-year program and met on Wednesdays and Sundays, but I didn't know this until I began my search for a synagogue. I needed a synagogue that would take him only for one year and only on Wednesdays. He couldn't attend on Sundays because our weekends were spent in Amagansett. The only shul that would accept him and give him a scholarship was Central Synagogue, a long-established Reform synagogue on the East Side. Reform was fine.

I had never thought about a Bat Mitzvah for Jody since there was no such thing for girls when I was growing up in Brownsville.

Ironically, like Nicky's grandfather in Europe, he, along with other boys in the class, questioned the existence of God. But instead of a slap across the mouth, a special class was created by the assistant rabbi to discuss the possibilities and probabilities of a God with these young would-be atheists.

Interestingly, we never had a God discussion at the dinner table. We talked about menstruation, birth control, sex, morality and politics, but we never had a discussion about God.

I came to regret that Nicky went to Hebrew School only for as long as he needed to become a bar mitzvah, and Jody didn't go at all. Nonetheless, we were cultural Jews and proud of our heritage.

16
The Sweetest Sixteen

The breakup of my marriage didn't mean ending my relationship with the Goodman family. I was very close to Phil's brother, Arnie, his wife Muriel, and was a doting aunt to Florence and Gina.

It was Gina's 16th birthday. Gina lived on Long Island in Levittown, went to high school, played the clarinet, hung out with friends, did her homework and enjoyed the fresh air and greenery of the exurbs. Other than coming in to visit for family celebrations, she probably came to New York two or three times in her entire life. I decided to change that. I drove to Levittown, picked her up, and we drove to New York City. Her birthday celebration had begun.

At this time my friend Ruth was doing the costumes for a film being shot on the Upper West Side in a small studio on Amsterdam Avenue. She invited us on the set. The name of the movie was "*Hot Rock*," about a group of inept hustlers who were going to steal a valuable diamond from the Brooklyn Museum. We watched a very funny scene of them planning their escapade. "Them" consisted of Zero Mostel, Paul Sand of The Second City Improv of Chicago, and yes, Robert Redford. Gina watched, enthralled.

At the break, Ruth introduced us and announced Gina's birthday. The fun began. They made a big fuss over her in true Hollywood fashion. Zero Mostel gave her a big bear hug, Paul Sand kissed her on both cheeks, and Robert Redford held her hand as they shouted, "Happy Birthday, Happy Birthday!" She was in a state of blissful shock when we left the set for dinner in a small neighborhood restaurant.

In 1968, Robert Redford was not yet a superstar. I told Gina that by the time the movie would be released, Robert Redford would be a big, big star. She said her friends would never believe he actually touched her.

Then there was the concert. Benny Goodman, of Swing fame, was giving a classical concert at Alice Tully Hall, and we had tickets. Gina had never been to a concert in New York, and she soaked up the music and the ambience. After the concert, an inspired Gina was preparing to leave.

"No," I said. "We're going backstage."

"We can't." She shrank back.

"Yes we can."

"No," she answered shyly.

"If we don't, how can he sign the clarinet reed you brought?"

She reluctantly followed me and like all teenagers was probably embarrassed by my adult behavior. At that time, not like in the theater or opera, anyone could go backstage after a concert. We got to Benny Goodman as he was talking to fans. At our turn, Gina was tongue-tied. I introduced us and told him Gina had ambitions to become the first woman clarinetist in the Philharmonic.

He looked down at her and smiled, "Really?"

"Yes," she shyly said and then found her voice.

"Will you sign my reed?"

He took her reed and as he signed it, he smiled again, "This is a first for me."

At this time, the Goodman Matzoh company sent buttons to all Goodmans in the metropolitan area which read, "With A Name Like Goodman, What Could Be Bad?" I was wearing my button. As Benny Goodman gave Gina the signed reed, I gave Benny Goodman my button.

It was the sweetest, sweet sixteen.

17
Whispers of Freedom

While producing "All About TV," Steve and I did a segment with the world-renowned photographer, Roman Vishniac, who chronicled Jewish life in Europe before the Holocaust. Appearing with him was Cornell Capa, the founder of the museum, The International Center of Photography, doing a segment called Photography in Peace.

Vishniac and I both lived on the Upper West Side, and after the show took the long ride home on the subway from the TV studio in the Municipal Building in downtown Manhattan. He told me about how, during World War II, he and about a hundred other Jews were forced to dig a deep pit, were then shot, fell backwards into the hole, and left for dead in the graves they had dug for themselves. He did not die, and after the massacre tried to crawl out from under the pile of dead bodies on top of him. A woman came along and saw movement. She helped him out and nursed him back to health; they later married. He said he forgave the Nazis. That was the past; now he had to get on with his life.

I was both deeply moved and astounded. Up to that point in my life, I said I would never go to Germany and would never, ever forgive the Nazis. It was unthinkable. But listening to his story, I came to the realization that if he could forgive the Nazis, after the horrors he had lived through, then certainly I should be able to do the same.

The question was how!

Vishniac told me the secret of freedom: forgiveness. I listened, heard intellectually, understanding for the first time it was the way to go, but emotionally could neither accept it nor take a step in that direction. I was stuck and couldn't move. Forget, maybe. Forgive? Never-never-never!

18
The Far East Beckons

Healing my sadness and anger was difficult. I was easily brought to tears and my anger would erupt quickly and at times inappropriately.

Help came unexpectedly. My friend Julie told me about a Japanese philosophy whose mantra had the power of healing and bringing prosperity. I needed help with both: money was a struggle and I still had a heavy heart. When you are drowning and someone throws you a rope, you grab it without asking whether it's hemp or a plastic facsimile. I grabbed it hard. Chanting the mantra took away some of the pain, and when Julie and her husband decided to go on a spiritual journey to Japan to the headquarters of the organization, I decided to go with them.

At this time, I knew an editor at *Time* magazine who warned me to keep my eyes and ears open. He even offered me an assignment to write about my experience. I assured him I fully intended to be vigilant. I hired my cleaning lady to help my parents with the children and off I went.

The trip turned out to be a fiasco. The head of the organization was a racist and an anti-Semite, calling Hawaiians "pineapple heads," making anti-Semitic slurs and trying to degrade Americans by giving us the most menial work, like cleaning toilets (which we actually did willingly). There were hidden cameras to spy on us. They billeted us on an open pier, filling it up with rows and rows of cots and calling it proper sleeping accommodations.

Julie, her husband and I left the group before the trip was over, making a stopover in Hawaii. I was heartbroken, having trusted and being let down again and spent most of the flight home crying. When I came back, I told my editor friend, "If I were writing the piece, I would call it, 'My Totalitarian Holiday,' but would not write the story under any circumstance for fear of my life." From what I saw and heard, I was not exaggerating.

This experience turned me off Eastern philosophies for a long, long time.

In 1980, at age 52, I was told by my friend Aviva about an Indian Guru touring the United States. Notwithstanding my past experience, my curiosity was aroused. I felt drawn to meet an Indian holy man and drove up to his ashram in the Catskills, not as a spiritual seeker but as someone who couldn't pass up the chance to see what an Indian Guru was like. How did he look? How did he behave? What did he teach?

Unwittingly, driving upstate that day, I had stumbled upon the most meaningful and fulfilling, yet challenging and difficult path that would change my life.

Part 2

The Forgiveness Journey

19
Initiation

The room was small. A man was giving a talk about his spiritual experiences when the back door opened. In walked the Guru, a short man with a big belly, dressed in orange robes and a big smile covering his face, emanating waves of power like I'd never experienced in my life before. He walked to his chair, sat down and began talking. His laughter, the twinkle in his eye, and spontaneous joy enchanted me.

I became a disciple.

Wanting to spend as much time with him as I could and thirsting for more knowledge of the teachings he imparted, I would go upstate to the Catskills ashram where he resided, for a weekend or a week's retreat. People were there from all over the world. I noticed that among my seven dorm roommates, there was usually one German. It was curious, and I was very uncomfortable, but it was bearable for the short term. As time went by I learned that everything in the ashram happened for a reason; there were no coincidences. I was being fed experiences of having Germans in my life in tiny baby steps. However, I still shuddered when I heard tourists speaking German on the bus in New York, and still vowed that I would never go to Germany.

Something indescribable happened at the ashram; something I find hard to explain. You thought nothing was happening or had happened. Life seemed to be about the same. But then you looked back on the year that had passed and found there had been a subtle shift. So it was with me and the Germans.

My feelings were changing imperceptibly, ever so slowly in tiny increments—less angry, less scared, less sad, less uncomfortable. Still, I shuddered when I heard German being spoken by tourists and reiterated my vow never to go to Germany.

According to the tradition of my Guru, a being like him could awaken your kundalini, or spiritual energy, which lay dormant at the base of the spine. Initiation could be transmitted by a touch, a look, or a thought. To have this experience, you could spend a special weekend with the Guru who I will call Babaji.

During that time, I was sad and weepy and felt too poor, too deprived to take this special weekend, particularly since Phil had just cheated me out of $800 he owed in child support. But while meditating, I had an insight. I felt if he could take money from me, I could turn it around and spend $150 on this occasion.

Standing on line waiting to get into the hall, I didn't know what to expect, except that whenever someone asked if it was my first and I said "Yes," they would smile and say "Ah" in such a way that I felt like a bride.

I sat in the dark with my eyes closed. As the Guru got closer, I smelled the incense and heard the swishing of his peacock-feathered wand. He pressed his thumb on my forehead between my eyes. I felt a wave of enormous masculine strength and unconditional love such as I never had before and began to weep with tears of joy and pain. I pleaded with Babaji silently from inside: "Please take away the tears. Enough tears. I'm tired of crying." With that, the flow of tears turned into two beautiful, gentle cascading waterfalls like the ones in the Finger Lakes in upstate New York where I had had many happy experiences. Then I saw a third eye inside my head. A beam of light was shooting out and another beam of light was pouring into my eye.

The meditation instructions were to go deeper inside and as I did, I saw square-colored clouds coming out in waves. They reminded me of wonderful paintings I had seen by the artists Ad Reinhardt and Joseph Albers. The squares moved off the canvas three-dimensionally into the universe and became the universe. I fell into that same happy, exquisite loving space which I knew, at that moment, was ME.

20
The Awakening

Years passed. I began my third career as Special Assistant to the New York State Commissioner of Human Rights, helped my children grow up and become young adults, tried to find a new life partner, remained active in local West Side politics, got older, and traveled the world to all seven continents. And in between, I was still mourning for what I had lost.

In October, 1982 Babaji left his physical body and Guruji became the Guru. In April, 1989 Guruji was leading a retreat in Heidelberg, Germany during Passover and Easter. I still had no intention of going—not to the retreat nor to Germany. I was standing at the office window of the New York ashram and overheard a devotee making plans to go to Heidelberg. The woman was an Israeli, pleasant but a bit of a flake. I turned to her, "Hava, are you going to Germany?" I asked incredulously. "Yes," she said. She looked into my eyes and said in a very serious voice, "Evelyn, you should come." The way she said it, so directly to me and so unlike her, made me feel as if the Guru was giving me a command and without thinking, I said, "yes."

Intuitively, I knew that I had to go to Germany and confront my demons. And while part of me knew that everything would be okay, another part of me was in a panic. I thought for sure I was going to my death. I wrote Guruji a letter telling her of my hysteria. To make sure she got it I sent a copy to the ashram in India and another to the center in Heidelberg. I was petrified and felt I couldn't go without her protection. My death was imminent.

For years, long before the publishing of the book and the release of the movie *"Schindler's List"* (the story of how Schindler, a German, saved Jews), I had been needing and wanting to know that there were Germans and other people in the world who did not hate Jews. I couldn't bear a reality that everyone in the world would ultimately hate me because I was Jewish.

As I prepared for my Heidelberg trip, my journey took on another dimension. I found books which told of the people of Assisi, Italy, who helped Jews while the German doctor in charge of the troops looked the other way, and of Polish farmers who hid Jews at their peril. I also found books about children of Nazis and their painful experiences of finding out what their fathers did. I took two of these books along with me as well as books by Babaji and Guruji about forgiveness and letting go. I was well fortified, but I was really, really scared. I felt I was going into the land of Hell, and I would be murdered.

When I visit a foreign country, I usually learn some basic words, trying to speak the language. But I had decided I would not speak German at all; I would make them speak English to me; I wouldn't meet anyone halfway. I knew Yiddish and had a year of German in college, so I understood quite a bit. At first, I was scared that if I tried to speak German they would immediately know I was Jewish. But then I realized that this was 1989 and that most younger people had regrettably never even heard Yiddish (their parents and grandparents made sure of that) and they would think I was speaking some dialect from the countryside. My next thought was that I was not going to hide that I was Jewish. I was going to drop my fear and stand proud.

I also knew that before I went to Heidelberg, I had to go to Dachau. I needed to see a death camp and, as much as I could, be in touch with what happened there.

I got off the plane in Munich with mixed emotions of fear, hatred and pain swirling inside me. I walked over to the information counter that had hotel listings. Behind the counter an elderly gentleman in his 60s, smiled at me and said, *"Guten Abend."* My inner voice sized him up and said, "And where were you during the war?" Instead, I answered, *"Guten Abend"* even though I had two big chips on my shoulders and was daring people to knock them off. He was very polite, friendly, got me what turned out to be a fine room, and gave me directions to the hotel.

That night was hell. I was delirious. I couldn't sleep. I took turns reading Babaji's and Guruji's books and then, reading about the German children, wept. Yes, I wept for Nazi children! Slept an hour or two, cried some more, and read about forgiveness and freedom. In my delirium, I spent the night pulled by emotions I couldn't control. The morning was sunny and bright, and after breakfast I went outdoors. Near the hotel was a pedestrian promenade. The first thing I saw was a fruit stand with fresh Israeli dates for sale! I bought a kilo and thought, "If the Israelis can make peace, why can't I?" I walked along the promenade and saw a large group of blond, young men in their teens in uniform drinking beer. I stopped to watch them. My mind went wild again. These were young Nazi SS cavorting in the street, and I shuddered. What would they do to me? One man came up to me and said with a big smile, "We're celebrating our release from the army today." I smiled back; the threat evaporated. Then an old man approached and started to speak in broken English. (I must have looked very American.) He had a paper in his hand and showed it to me, beaming. It was a map of America. He said, in very broken English, "I am to America going to my brother to visit. He lives in America," and pointed to Milwaukee. A spontaneous smile came to my face. Another fear left me and for a moment I almost began to enjoy my walk to the train station and Dachau.

Dachau was a station on the U-Bahn, a train system both above and below ground. The train to Munich was above ground. It was eerie and scary, to say the least. I was riding on a train—destination Dachau—passing empty freight cars on adjacent tracks—freight cars that once took Jews to Dachau and their death. An hour out of Munich, the train stopped at a small station: the sign read DACHAU.

I got off and found another sign saying the camp was about a kilometer down the main road. The houses I passed were small—white with yellow, blue, pink, or green shutters. Sweet, neat, clean, and antiseptic. I wanted to shout, "Open your shutters! Don't tell me you didn't know. You could smell the stench of burning corpses. Don't look so innocent. Of course you knew!"

I arrived at the camp. The gates with their infamous slogan, *Arbeit Macht Frei* (Work Makes You Free), were open.

I entered a building and the first thing that greeted me was a dark wall about 16-feet long. On it was a huge map of Europe with a dot denoting where there had been a concentration camp. I was amazed at just how many there were. The map looked like a star-filled sky. Only they weren't stars; they were death camps.

I overheard two men talking, recognized they were American, and easily joined their conversation. They were TWA pilots, non-Jews, who were studying the Third Reich, and needed, like me, to visit a camp. It was a relief to be able to have company, like-minded company, to share out loud my feelings of horror and pain as I walked through the museum and camp. In a corner of the tranquil park-like grounds, were two open-doored ovens with the familiar-looking, ominous chimneys. In one oven, someone had placed a lone rose. At one point we were shown a film and before it started, I took out the Israeli dates, shared them with the pilots and toasted *L'Chayim* (to Life). They toasted me for my bravery in coming alone.

After about an hour, we left Dachau, and the pilots, Mac and Tom, invited me to have a drink in Munich. To me Munich meant Hitler's *Putsch*—one of the first violent acts by Hitler's thugs. They drank in the beer halls, brawled, and took over the police station. The beer hall we went to reeked of beer and could easily have been one of those same places. Since the pilots were on the wagon and the hall gave me the creeps, we decided to leave.

We walked around Munich in the same pedestrian mall I had investigated the day before. Mac said that in his studies Germany had no plaques about the Third Reich anywhere in the country; they were outlawed. As we walked, I noticed an empty lot between two buildings that seemed out of place. Looking closely, I found a plaque saying it commemorated the location of the police station Hitler's henchmen had destroyed that long time ago.

We walked and talked some more until we got to the train station. They again told me how brave I had been to come alone, and I told them I was not really alone. I was with them, and I felt protected by my Guru. Tom, the younger one, the single one, invited me to come to Berlin. I invited him to come to Heidelberg.

From Munich to Heidelberg was another train ride. The Munich station was big with many platforms and of course the announcements were in German. What I didn't know was that my train had been changed to another track, and had I not been talking to a woman on the platform waiting for the same train, I would have missed the train to Heidelberg. On the train was a young man in my compartment who spoke English and kept me company during the entire trip. Again, the universe had provided me with a protective shield. Talking to him helped calm me down a little, but my heart and mind were still racing. I only quieted down when I got to the Heidelberg retreat center and the safety of my Guru.

The center was filled with people from all over Europe. It was not only Passover, but also Good Friday and April Fool's Day. While we were all being very serious about our time with the Guru, she was laughing and playing April Fool's jokes on us. The program started. As usual, she welcomed everyone with respect and love and then spoke to the host country, Germany. She talked about how industrious, clean, disciplined, and fierce the Germans were (fierce was her only reference to the past).

She began telling a story. As she told it, I felt, even though there were a thousand people in the hall, that she was looking directly at me. Each word penetrated me. She told of a man who came up to his Guru pleading with him to show him God. The Guru told him, "Come back tomorrow with a large sack, and fill it with three huge rocks." He did so and returned. "Now," said the Guru, "Take the sack, with these rocks, and climb this mountain."

I knew she was talking to me, and I began to cry, sobbing with recognition and pain. The words shot through me. I couldn't stop crying. She went on: "The man climbed a while and got very tired. "Throw out one of the rocks," said the Guru. The man did so, climbed some more until he could barely move. "Throw out another rock." He continued climbing until he felt he couldn't go another step further, although he was almost at the top. "Throw out the last rock." He did as commanded. Exhausted, he reached the top and crawled to his master's feet. "Now will you show me God?' Through my sobbing I heard the answer, "Do you think you could have climbed this mountain, carrying those rocks, without God?"

Still weeping, I fell into deep meditation. From the top of my head came huge iron and steel chunks of scrap metal. Heavy scrap from the junkyard—twisted cars, cranes, unrecognizable pieces of steel—poured out. They just kept coming and coming. It seemed endless: a volcanic eruption of heavy, heavy debris pouring out of my head. I watched in amazement. It went on for I don't know how long, and then it stopped. When I came out of meditation, I felt like a roto rooter had scrubbed my insides: weightless, light, and clean. I felt happy and prayed for this feeling to continue forever!

Then I had a huge breakthrough. I realized that the same hatred, bitterness, anger, sadness and pain that I was carrying for the Germans, I was also carrying for Phil! It was coloring all my relationships and eating into my gut. I was stunned. I now knew I had to forgive not only the Germans, but my ex-husband as well! But how could I forgive the unforgivable? After meditation, I went up for *darshan*, the time devotees greet the Guru and traditionally offer fruit, flowers, or money. I had brought chocolate-covered matzohs and macaroons with me, anticipating the possibility of sharing Passover with the Germans. As I gave the Guru my Passover goodies as an offering, I said, "It's the first night of Passover as well as Easter," and thought to myself, "I will not be at a seder (traditional Passover dinner) this year, but that's okay." The next day, in meditation, I was at my dining room table having a seder. Seated on my left were my daughter, son-in-law and his parents. Directly opposite me was the Guru and my great, great, great grandfather, Rebbe Levi Yitzhak of Berditchev. To the right was my ex-husband and my ex-enemies, and all the Germans in the hall. I served Passover vegetarian goodies to the Guru and the Rebbe and then to everyone. The table got bigger and bigger to accommodate all the Germans at the retreat and in Germany. It got even bigger until there was seating space to include everyone in the whole world. Everyone was at my seder table! It was the best seder I ever had in my whole life!

During the sharing session, I shared my meditation experience. Germans came up to me later to tell me their stories. Some knew they were children of Nazis; some had just found out they were. Some had one Jewish and one German parent, or they had just found out about their parents' involvement with the Nazi regime and were ashamed. They cried. I cried. Teary-eyed, I was able to hug them and share their pain and my matzohs and macaroons. I knew then I would never say "never" again and that my forgiveness journey had begun!

To top it off, Tom did come to Heidelberg to see me. He got to meet the Guru, and I even had a date.

21
The Challenge

Unbeknownst to me, Heidelberg set me up for a monumental cosmic joke. The following year, my son-in-law Fred, who was considering an assignment in Israel with his company, instead accepted a posting to Germany for a four-year stint. Of all the countries in the world it had to be Germany! Had he taken Israel I would have rented a house and lived there for a year, something I had always wanted to do. Reluctantly, I made plans to visit Fred and Jody in Bonn and then Berlin, where they moved when Berlin became the capital of a unified Germany.

Luckily, some of my irrational fears had been buried earlier at the Heidelberg retreat. My next visit had to be easier. With the birth of Betsy, my granddaughter, I paid four more visits to Germany, and being with family, each visit was with a little less trepidation, apprehension, and fear. I was somewhat more comfortable but still conflicted.

Could I meet the challenge? What would it take to forgive? How far would I have to go before this stuff—or as the Germans would say *Schmutz* (dirt)—would go away?

Does it ever really go away?

22
Forgiveness—What It Is and What It Is Not

Forgiveness is not letting the person off the hook for doing something despicable. It's not saying, "It's okay. I forgive you." It's not okay. It isn't forgetting the trauma. It happened. You were hurt! It's not negating the pain. It's not becoming friends or even liking the person. It's not going back to the same relationship and allowing yourself to be hurt again. Most importantly, it has nothing to do with the person not deserving to be forgiven, or that he hasn't asked for forgiveness. Wait to hear the words "I'm sorry" and you'll never forgive. It has to do with *you. You deserve it!*

What is forgiveness? As Louise Hay says, "Forgiveness is self-love." It is letting go of the pain of yesterday and opening yourself up to the joy of today and tomorrow.

For me it was having the sorrow, the hatred, the bitterness and the pain leave. It was having the anger, which was the size of a basketball lodged in my gut, shrink slowly over many years to the size of a peach pit.

It's freedom. It's being light. I no longer have the physical weight of the feelings of victimization, self-pity and self-righteousness inside me. I feel as if I'm walking around in a cloud of free-floating euphoria, and it feels great.

How do I express that self-love? Every time a negative emotion comes up, I don't fight it. I acknowledge it with love and say, "You were once a part of me. Now, you serve no purpose. I no longer need you. I send you on your way—out of my psyche and out of my life."

It is a mysterious mixture of determination, hard work, and a wise therapist, stirred by the finger of God.

To the atheists and agnostics among you, please don't close the book and walk away. As a former *devout* atheist, let me reassure you that I don't believe in the same God you don't believe in. God is not an old man with a long white beard sitting on a throne meting out punishment.

God is Consciousness, a Higher Power, a Divine Mystery, transcendent and immanent, a creative force infusing all of life.

I came to believe this, not because someone convinced me of the error of my ways, but because I *experienced* it. Experience cannot be argued away. As Carl Jung said, "I don't believe, I know." For me, God is Love, dwelling in each of us, as close to us as our breath.

23
First Steps

The phone rang. It was Phil! He wanted to talk to me.

"Could we meet at the local coffee shop this afternoon? Is three o'clock okay?"

"Sure," I said, wondering what he wanted. What was he up to?

I arrived promptly to find Phil sitting in a booth. I sat down while doing the perfunctory hellos.

"You look great," he said, trying to charm me. He didn't charm me; he disgusted me.

I asked matter of factly, "What do you want?"

Jody was getting married in a few months, and he wanted to talk to me about the upcoming celebrations. Amidst the excitement of planning the wedding was my concern that Jody would invite the babysitter, who was now living with Phil. I didn't want her to but felt I couldn't tell Jody not to invite her. I would be very upset if she were there, but I also knew it would be a big mistake to demand Jody not invite her.

Instead, I told Jody: "If Shelly is invited it will spoil my entire day."

Phil said Jody told him to settle this between us. She was not taking sides.

"I'd like to have Michelle at the wedding" (she was now calling herself by her grown-up name).

I was adamant and said frostily, "If she were your wife I'd have no alternative. But she's not your wife (I didn't say what I wanted to say, 'She's your whore') and I don't want her at the wedding." Phil got angry and threatened, "Then I'll tell Jody I won't invite any of my friends."

"That's up to you."

And then, out of the blue, the words came blurting out of my mouth, "I forgive you." What a shock. Did those words come from *my* lips?

He looked up surprised, "Michelle, too?" He asked.

Begrudgingly, with a shrug I said, "Her too."

"You forgive me," he said. "How wonderful for me."

"No," I replied. "How wonderful for me."

I knew I had a long way to go but it was a big step forward. Even though I didn't fully mean it or believe it, the words had come out. I was able to say them even though I only partially meant it.

Could I ever *really* mean it? I doubted it.

24
On the Road

It was May, and I was in Amagansett with my camera and Betsy Cameron's book *"The Artists' Way,"* starting my 10-day stay at the house before the summer tenants moved in. I was looking forward to walking on the beach, going to art openings, eating yummy bay scallops and fresh veggies from the Farmer's Market, picking strawberries, watching sunsets (no sunrise person me), going to the movies and seeing Amagansett friends, when I got a frantic phone call from Jody.

"Could you please help?" It was Grandparents' Day at Betsy's school, and there was nobody who could come.

"Could you please come?"

Of course I would.

I dropped everything and readied myself for the five-hundred mile drive to Washington. For some reason, my friend Marilyn and I had exchanged cars. Her car had a burglar alarm so efficient that it went off at all times, usually inappropriately. After our last midnight episode, she took the car to her mechanic who physically disconnected the alarm. The wiring was still there, but it could no longer disturb the neighborhood.

I was enjoying the drive and anticipating a visit with my delicious four-year-old granddaughter. I made good time. Half-way there, at the Delaware Memorial Bridge, I made a pit stop. I turned off the ignition and to my horror the disconnected alarm went off! I couldn't get it to stop wailing!

I found a pay phone (these were the days before cell phones) and tried calling Marilyn at the school where she taught. I left a message for her to call me back. I also called the Automobile Association of America. I shuttled back and forth frantically from the phone to the place where I could see the AAA truck.

I turned to a man standing near the phone.

"Could you please answer the phone if it rings and call me?"

"*Ich spreche kein Englisch, aber ich kann meinen Bruder rufen.*" (I don't speak English, but I'll call my brother.")

His brother came over, and from his accent I could tell he was a German-American. I told him my problem with the car and that I needed the phone to get help.

He broke into a smile, "I had the same trouble with my car. I can fix it. "

"Really? I asked incredulously.

"Really." He nodded his head "yes," still smiling. I showed him where my car was, told him the license number, gave him the keys and off he went. He came back in about 10 minutes, still smiling. "Everything is OK." He had silenced the monster.

I thanked him profusely. His hand shook when he returned the keys. All choked up, he said, "You trusted me. You trusted me with the keys to your car."

"Of course."

We shook hands as he returned the keys. I drove on to Washington to a wonderful visit with Betsy.

To this day I have no logical explanation why the car alarm went off.

25
An Eerie Night

It was a misty, foggy summer night in Amagansett at the seashore; the air was still and foreboding but yet beautiful. The street lamp in front of the house was shrouded in fog. It was mysteriously eerie.

I walked outside into the mist. The air smelled sweet and wet. The scent enveloped me as I began walking from one lamp to the next. I enjoyed the feeling of freedom and yet I felt as if I was being pulled by a power beyond my control.

I started walking down the road from lamp to lamp toward the ocean. I walked as if in a dream, recognizing the trees, yet not. I couldn't see the moon; the hazy lamplights made me feel as if they were the moon.

I heard the waves breaking gently, and I kept walking, crossing the road that led to the ocean. The ocean got louder as I got closer and its rhythmic sound was both soothing and hypnotic. I found myself on the beach, still being pulled as if by a magnetic force.

The thick mist, parting only intermittently, kept me from seeing the moon, but I felt its presence. I was being drawn into the ocean. I stood mesmerized at the water's edge, and had I not been fully conscious, I do believe I could have walked into the ocean without ever looking back.

26
Language of the Heart—The Whales of Baja

If there were such a thing as a next lifetime, I would choose to come back either as a First Amendment lawyer or a marine biologist. I've tried to make these dreams come true in this lifetime, and live life to its fullest, which maybe explains why I became the Special Assistant to the Commissioner of the New York State Division of Human Rights and went on many trips all over the world to see animals and marine life.

One of these trips was to the Baja Peninsula in Mexico to be with the grey whales and their calves in Magdalena Bay. These magnificent 70,000 pound, 45-foot creatures spend the summer in the waters of the Bering and Chukchi Seas of Alaska, then swim the roughly 5,000-mile journey down the Pacific Coast to the Baja lagoons of Mexico where they breed and give birth. When born, the calves are about 15 feet long and weigh anywhere from one to one and a half tons. They nurse for about five months to the tune of about 12 gallons of milk a day; the males are excluded from this maternal scene. They wait patiently, or not so patiently, in the ocean outside the lagoon for the females to be available as mates again as they head out for the trip north.

I stayed with a group of eighteen Elder Hostelers on a small and uninhabited island in the bay, where tents were pitched and campsites set up. And every day after breakfast we divided into three groups and went out in small motor boats to play with the whales. We didn't need to look for them; they seemed to be waiting to play as they swam out to meet our boats.

One whale got under our boat and spun us around. It was as if she were showing us who was boss. With one movement of her head she could have flipped us over, but instead chose to play. Another dove under and over us, splashing as we applauded. I watched some people in another boat bending over the side trying to touch a whale. The whale teased them. Every time they thought they were close enough to touch, she went further down into the water, just out of reach.

As I watched the whales, I felt very humble, not merely because of their power but because I felt they were teaching us. Teaching us about forgiveness. After all, it was only 85 years ago that we were slaughtering these intelligent mammals and almost causing their extinction. I do believe they have communicated this history to their offspring. Yet, here they were, with humans, frolicking in the water like delighted children acting as if nothing had ever happened.

In my new practice of meditation I was given a Sanskrit mantra, which means, "I honor my Inner Self; I bow to the Divine that dwells within me." My plan for this trip was to share the mantra with the whales. I wanted not only to create a bond with this intelligent species, but also to share a message of oneness which I felt they would understand. For me, it was a gesture of love and a request for forgiveness.

I brought a recording of the mantra being chanted by the Guru, turned it on and placed it about two inches above the water knowing that sound traveled easily in water. It had been playing for about five minutes when I spotted a whale and her baby at the far end of the lagoon. She began swimming toward the boat, baby in tow. She was heading directly toward me and the mantra. When she reached the boat, she put her head out of the water, looked at me and raised her baby up to me. I reached my hand out toward her and she allowed me to touch her baby! Its skin was rough and its body throbbed with life. It was thrilling! She and the baby went below the surface and then came up again. The mother raised her up to my fingers, and I was allowed to touch the baby again. It was no accident! It was an acknowledgement of a message received!

I was silent, thrilled and moved to tears during this amazing interchange. After they swam away, I sat frozen in a state of privileged joy and ecstasy. I felt as if I had made a cosmic friend; I had found family. When I left Mexico for home, I felt sadness and joy at the same time. It was one of the most remarkable experiences of my life.

There is a back story. For some years before my magical encounter, Mitsubishi and the Mexican Government had been planning to build salt mines in this very bay, which would have destroyed the breeding ground of the grey whales. The Natural Resources Defense Council, an environmental agency, had been fighting this project and I, as a member of this dedicated organization, had sent letters and signed petitions to both parties, but to no avail. The plans were continuing, even though by now the NRDC announced there was to be a boycott of Mitsubishi.

A few weeks after I got home, I received a letter from Mitsubishi saying the project wasn't their doing, but rather that of their parent corporation. A month later, I received another letter saying, without explanation, the project was being abandoned! No salt mines!

I felt not only did I make new friends, but I played a part in saving their lives.

27
The New York Marathon

My first case as Special Assistant involved the 1978 New York Marathon. It was a small race then and fairly new to the New York scene. Bobby Hall, a paraplegic, who won the 1975 Boston Marathon in a wheelchair, wanted to run in New York but was told by Fred Lebow, the head of the New York Road Runners, it was only for able-bodied people who could use their legs. It was not for wheelchair participants; they weren't athletes like the Greeks of old.

Bobby Hall, and another marathon wheelchair runner from Provo, Utah, filed a complaint stating they were prevented from participating in the New York Marathon because they were in wheelchairs. I found in their favor, stating since NYC streets were used for the Marathon, all persons who wished to should be able to participate. The Human Rights Division's Administrative Law Judge upheld the ruling but the Road Runners took the case to court where the decision was overturned. We lost, but Mayor Koch had the last word. He ruled that as long as the Marathon was run on city streets, it should be open to all.

My role was to make sure that on the day of the event the wheelchairs were started in a timely fashion and were at the finish line without interference. The race started on the Verrazano Bridge, across to Brooklyn and Queens, into the Bronx and Harlem, winding up in Central Park.

I, the non-athlete, who greatly admired all runners, got as close to a marathon as I ever would. I started in the early, early a.m. and was on the bridge overlooking New York Harbor. In the early light, way, way down, I could see boats looking like tiny toys floating in a vast bathtub of blue. The sun hadn't come up yet and the gray of the early morning made me feel as if I was a cumulus cloud hovering over the bay.

On the bridge, the runners were quietly warming up, exercising, tying their sneakers, one-pointedly preparing to run the best race they knew how. I was very inspired observing them, realizing the body can be pushed beyond its limits and how much can be accomplished by hard work and determination.

Starting time came and off they went—the wheelchairs first—and then the swarm of human bodies covering the entire bridge. It was awesome.

I was at the finish line to cheer the wheelchairs on and to make sure their race was properly recorded. The crowd was wildly cheering them, feeling differently from Lebow and his narrow-minded notion of what an athlete really was.

The marathon is now huge, has over 50,000 runners coming from all over the world to participate, and the wheelchair athletes are a permanent fixture in the race.

It made me think of the cerebral palsy kids I taught one year in elementary school. Boys in wheelchairs, feeling they were prisoners in their chairs, who had no thoughts of becoming athletes, let alone participating in a race with able-bodied people. Now they no longer feel less than; they have role models and hope.

28
Radiance

I was on a trip with the Society for the Advancement of Judaism to a place I thought I would never ever see—the grave of Rabbi Levi Yitzhak of Berditchev, my great, great, great grandfather.

It was sunny, everything was green and lush but overgrown that day in July 2004, as we walked through the gate of the old Jewish cemetery in Berditchev, Ukraine. A small hut-like building housed the Rebbe's grave. Vandals had desecrated the gravestone some years earlier, and the hut was built to protect the new stone. Miraculously, the grave had survived World War II, the Nazis, and the Communists. Inside was an old man sitting on a chair, whose loving *mitzvah* (commandment) it was to watch over the grave. I went up to him and said in Yiddish: "*Ikh bin ein enkel fun der Berditchever*" (I am a grandchild of the Berditchever).

He smiled, looked me full in the face and said, "*Gut gezunt auf dir. Gutgezunt auf dine kinder. Gut gezint auf dine enechlach*" (Good health to you. Good health to your children. Good health to your grandchildren.) His words went through me, and I got goose bumps. I felt at that moment, with those words, the Rebbe himself was blessing me, my family and everyone with me.

It is customary, at the grave of a great Rebbe, to leave a written *kvitil* (note) at his gravesite. Legend has it that the wish will be granted. I put my *kvitil*, and the *kvitil* I brought with me from my friends, on the gravestone. Interestingly, none of my Jewish friends gave me any; my Christian meditation yogic friends did. In my *kvitil*,

I thanked the Rebbe for being with me in my everyday life. And I asked that I be with him. I asked for union.

I knelt at the grave, put my head on it, and kissed it. I held it and through my fingertips, enveloped it. My eyes were closed, and I opened myself up to the Rebbe's presence. I breathed in the silence and the beauty of the moment. I asked for health, courage, wisdom and strength for me and everyone in my life to be able to deal with whatever came along.

Enveloped in the experience, I heard the beautiful voice of our rabbi, Michael Strassfeld, singing a *niggun* (a wordless prayer). We all spontaneously joined in and made a sound both mournful and joyous. It was powerful. I closed my eyes and saw the Rebbe smiling and dancing on his grave, like Hassidim do, clapping and throwing his arms in the air in ecstasy. I blinked, and he was gone. I closed my eyes, and there he was again, laughing and dancing. I could tell by his smile that Michael's singing pleased the Rebbe, and again, my entire body felt the electrical charge of his energy blessing us. I felt the room light up with his love, embracing us all. Michael touched the grave with his prayer book for a blessing and when I told him what I saw, he smiled and nodded. I knew he understood.

Near the gravesite was a small sanctuary, and it was there that another dream of mine came true. Levi Yitzhak wrote his teachings in a two-volume book, *"Kedushah Levi."* I own the books. They are on my bookshelf. I touch them, I dust them, and I feel their energy. But I cannot read them; I do not know Hebrew. I feel that even if I learn Hebrew, I will not read well enough to penetrate the teachings. With Michael translating that day at the gravesite, we all studied from *"Kedushah Levi."* Being at the Rebbe's grave, hearing his words directly from his own writings, was a very precious moment in time for me—a gift I will always cherish with deep gratitude. When we were outdoors again in the sunshine, Michael sang the *Kaddish* (prayer for the dead) with us, and I read some of the eulogies that poured from the Jewish world at the time of his death in 1809.

According to the account in Samuel Dresner's book, *"The Life of a Hasidic Master-Levi Yitzhak of Berditchev"*: "Everywhere among scholars of the Torah and simple people alike there was weeping and lamentation—a feeling that there had been taken from them the very Arc of the Lord. Both men and women, young and old, wept that the Holy One of Berditchev was no longer."

Those Hasidim who lived in Berditchev or journeyed there, as great numbers did to be present at the funeral procession, claimed they saw a pillar of fire going before the coffin.

When Rabbi Nachman of Bratzlav, who referred to the Rabbi of Berditchev as "the Glory of Israel," heard of the death and funeral, he said, "Surely it is possible that there is a pillar of light going before his coffin, for the true leader of Israel has died. He who has eyes in his head knows that the light has gone from the world and darkness has enveloped us all."

Indeed, it is told that at the very hour Rabbi Yitzhak died, a *Tzaddik* (a righteous one) teaching in a distant city suddenly interrupted his discourse, in which he was trying to fuse the power of doctrine with that of worship, and said to his disciples,"I cannot go on. Everything has become dark before my eyes. The gates of prayer are closing. Something must have happened to the great worshiper—Rabbi Levi Yitzhak."

During the weeks following his death, eulogies were delivered for Levi Yitzhak in many communities by the *Tzaddikim* of that time. Some said that while the loss of the great luminary had brought darkness and misery to all Israel, it had brought light and gladness to the Upper Worlds. They explained this by referring to the verse in the *Book of Ecclesiastes*, "A time for mourning and a time for dancing." For in truth, light and darkness, mourning and rejoicing, were intermingled at that moment.

Mourning and darkness in the Lower World.

Dancing and light in the Upper World.

Since the death of Levi Yitzhak, Berditchev has had no rabbi. No one could be found to take his place.

29
Thanksgiving's Unexpected Goodies

In my family, for me, Thanksgiving was an every-other-year celebration. Jody did not want both me and Phil at the table together; she felt there was still too much acrimony. Although I had told her for years we could now be cordial to each other, she would not accept it.

In order for me to heal, the next Thanksgiving, on my turn, I was encouraged by my therapist to invite Phil to come along—a specific giving up of my time alone with the family. The idea was repugnant to me. Why should he share my infrequent, sweet, valued time with my daughter and grandchildren, particularly when I felt he and "her" (the sitter he now lived with) spent more time with my family than I did?

But slowly, slowly, I began to feel more comfortable with the idea of sharing the time, even though I put myself in a very vulnerable position. I was not as good a storyteller, nor as charming, nor as "Pied Piperish" as he and relived the old feelings of coming out second best. I put that all behind me. Feeling comfortable and secure in who I am, I tried to convince Jody that it was okay to invite her father. We *could* spend the holiday together. And this time, perhaps because he was just diagnosed with prostate cancer, she not only said yes but asked a favor. Since she didn't have room in her house for her in-laws and me and Phil, she asked if I could please go to a hotel and give my room to her father.

"He has just finished his last round of chemo and is vulnerable," she said. I was caught by surprise; it certainly wasn't as much of an intimate warm visit being in a hotel room. It also was inconvenient for me since I didn't have a car. I hesitated for just a moment and then said, "Yes. Sure."

I was somewhat apprehensive about the weekend. One day was one thing, but spending a weekend with Phil was not exactly my idea of a good time. It's different from just a dinner. I must say I had other trepidations as well. Could I control myself and not call him on his lies and exaggerations? Could I control my emotions when he bragged about himself at others' and maybe my expense? Would I be sad? Repulsed? Happy? I was risking a lot, but it was worth it. As painful as it would be, I knew this was another step toward freedom.

Thanksgiving arrived. Jody was cooking and we were all sitting in the kitchen chatting. I turned to Phil, the writer-director, and told him I had started writing and was very excited about it. He looked shocked.

"You're writing? I have a rival." I smiled and thought, as usual, it's all about him.

"No Phil, I'm not your rival."

"What are you writing—prose or poetry?"

"I'm writing my memoir."

"I don't want to rain on your parade, but unless it's brilliant, only your friends and relatives will read it."

"I don't care. I don't care if no one reads it. I'm writing for myself, and I'm loving it."

"Ah. You've learned the secret of writing. It took me a long time to learn that."

He then thanked me very much for taking the hotel room and offered to pay for it.

"You're very welcome," I said, accepting his offer. Turning to Jody, he thanked her for inviting him. I wanted to set the record straight and said, "It was my idea to invite you."

He started getting weepy. "I asked to be invited. I'm old, I'm sick, blah, blah, blah. It's important to be with my kids. They are so great."

"I know. That's why I invited you."

In melodramatic tones, he said how much he loved his children and how they were all he lived for. I bit my tongue. I remembered that after I had two miscarriages and was desperate for a child, he announced he didn't want to have children. (Years later he told me it was because he was having an affair). I remembered that I was distraught and that my gynecologist told me to leave him. Still in love with him and now 28 years old, with my biological clock ticking, I couldn't leave him. Instead, I tricked him. I told him I was not ovulating, which I was; we welcomed in the new year by making love. Nine months later Jody was born.

Instead of saying this out loud, I asked him what he was working on. He seemed embarrassed.

"My old play about my father. It was only one act."

"I remember. It was good. It wasn't three acts because you never finished it."

"I was told by Lee Strasberg that it was a gem, so good. That really scared me. Would you like to read it?" he asked.

I eagerly said, "Yes." I really did want to read it. I was curious to see how or if he had changed.

He went on monopolizing the conversation with his mixture of braggadocio and self-pity. At the same time he was bragging about the musical he wrote with a very talented composer, he shared that the composer refused to allow him at rehearsals, because he was disruptive.

I listened to him talk about his good friends of 40 years, the harem of females who were attached to him. He told us that Eva, the widow of his best friend Nick, reminded him that he advised Nick not to marry her. She was *still* angry.

"It was the duty of the best man—me—to remind Nick of the pitfalls of marriage."

He told one story after another about how he was rejected or insulted or not appreciated. He told me how Naomi Duckler, the wife of an old mutual friend from the drama department at Brooklyn College who lived in L.A., called him, chatted a few moments and then instead of asking to see him, asked for my phone number.

"I would have made time to see her," he said. "I'm not that important. But they wanted to see *you*," he said to me. I bit my tongue again and said nothing, but I sure was tempted to say maybe they liked me more than you. His lying, bragging and putting himself down was the same conversation I lived with for 17 years and was exactly what I needed to hear now. I was free of this and ecstatic he was no longer in my life.

We have a ritual on Thanksgiving that by now has become a tradition. Fred's parents and brother bring pies from what we consider to be the best bakeries in New York to Washington. Jody and the children also bake pies. We taste and judge the pies, sometimes as many as a dozen. We take this pie-tasting contest very seriously, and review the pies as if we were reviewing Tennessee Williams or Arnold Schoenberg. With four writers and intelligent teenagers in the room, we laugh a lot as we taste, discard or embrace the pies with profound critique. That year's crop was disappointing.

Ross (age 17): "What are the symptoms of salmonella? This is just too unsafe to eat."

Saul (Fred's brother, age 50): "Not since kindergarten did I have so much fun with clay."

Harwood (Fred's father): "It tastes like wood fillers."

Jody (age 54): "Understated."

Wynona (Fred's mother): "Medicinal."

Yael (age 16): "Like when you try to swallow cough medicine."

Noa (age 12): "Aftertaste of stale goldfish."

Fred (Age 54): "Dentist office toothpaste."

But some pies got good reviews. (Jody's home-baked actually won.)

Betsy (age 21): "Delicious edge. Good spicing. Good texture."

Me: "A pie with potential."

And then Phil's inappropriate showstopper: "It tastes like a French kiss."

I quietly excused myself and ran to the bathroom. I ran the water in the sink, closed the lid on the commode, sat down and flushed the toilet so I couldn't be heard shouting, with my hands in the air, "Thank you, God. I'm so grateful I'm no longer married to him. He's no longer in my life. Thank you. Thank you. I'm free to be me."

30
Height / Weight

Jose R. wanted to be a policeman from the time he was a little kid. He couldn't wait to grow up. When he finally did grow up, it was to 5'6", not tall enough for the New York Police Department's requirement of 5'7".

But Jose wasn't giving up on his dream that easily and came to my office at the Division of Human Rights to file a complaint. The Division was set up as a legal entity to implement the New York State Human Rights Law without resorting to the overcrowded courts.

In the course of my investigation, I discovered there was no particular reason for the height qualification except that it had always existed. It was not a Bona Fide Occupational Qualification (BFOQ); it was just historical. Also, the height qualification had an adverse impact on Hispanics and women. It didn't discriminate directly, but had the unintentional consequence of denying them employment.

Jose had passed all the other parts of the test, and I found in his favor. He was entitled to the job as long as he could do it. The height requirement was not necessary for the job; it was not a BFOQ. Jose R. not only became a police officer but helped open the door to Hispanics and women.

Whenever I am at a parade or a police barricade where police officers are just standing around, I tell a female or a Hispanic officer about the case and how I got the qualifications changed. I usually get a big smile, a handshake, and a thank you. Sometimes they ask fellow officers to hear the story.

It makes me feel good to know I helped changed the look of the NYPD.

And then there was girth.

Charlie W. came to my office; he too wanted to be a police officer. He was huge. He stood at 5'10" and appeared to weigh between 250 and 300 pounds. The Police Department turned him down because of his weight.

I asked him, "What will your duties be?"

He replied, "I'll be in the Traffic Department, and I'll walk up and down the street giving tickets."

"What's your work now?" I asked.

"I work in a warehouse as big as a city block and walk back and forth with merchandise all day."

I nodded. "Tell me, what do you do for recreation?"

He broke into a huge grin. "I love to dance. I go to a disco two or three nights a week."

I grinned in return and found in his favor.

The NYPD now has obese police officers and maybe some even dance on the job.

31
Still on the Road

In 2010, I found a spiritual trip I very much wanted to make. It was on a small cruise ship to Mexico, where we would be immersed in the teachings and also have free time to explore Mexico. How perfect!

Except that I couldn't find someone to go with. My friend Sydell wanted to go, but was not well enough. She suggested Karen, a friend of hers I didn't know. Karen and I talked on the phone, met, decided we were a good fit and would take the trip together.

She was German. I told her I had had a life-changing experience in Germany and that I would tell her about it when we had time. She was anxious to hear my story, but somehow, with all the fascinating experiences on the retreat and in Mexico, we never did get the time.

We just became friends.

I do believe that such a close encounter with a German could not have happened without the beneficence of a Higher Power continuing to unlock the inner strength I did not know I possessed.

32
The Efficacy of the Mantra

It was January 1991, and I was in India at the ashram on my way to Bonn, Germany, to visit Jody and newborn baby Betsy. Just before I was to leave, I injured my back badly and could hardly walk. Stu Marmorstein, the wonder-man chiropractor, put me back together just enough to enable me to manage the long plane ride to Germany.

I could handle the back pain, but I was very worried about handling my luggage. I was taking a train from the airport in Frankfurt to Dusseldorf to be met by Jody and possibly Fred, for the drive to Bonn. What was going to happen to my suitcase? I could hardly walk, let along manage a suitcase. Jody, having just given birth, was certainly not able to lift anything heavy.

What was going to happen on the train platform? I was very concerned and went to one of the swamis for advice. What he said intrigued me, "From now on, send the mantra to the train platform. Keep visualizing the situation with the mantra in it. The mantra can change the dynamic." I was fascinated and could see the possibilities. In any case, I had no alternative. From that moment on, and for the next few days until I left the ashram, I repeated the mantra while sending it ahead to Dusseldorf.

I got to Dusseldorf and got off the train. Except for a young male gypsy stretched out on a bench asking, *"Haben Sie ein klein bissel Geld?* (Do you have a little bit of money?)," the platform was empty. There was nobody there to meet me!

After my initial moment of panic, I got to a pay phone and called Fred's office. I spoke to his assistant, who immediately came to the station, took care of me and my suitcase and drove me to Jody's house.

Nobody was home! They were at the pediatrician's office on an emergency visit. Fred thought there was something wrong with baby Betsy and took her and Jody to the doctor. When they arrived back home they were surprised to see me.

Fred took care of Betsy, but I was taken care of as well.

The mantra worked! Very mysteriously and in an unexpected way, the mantra worked!

33
Alaska

Middle to late August is a good time to visit Alaska, when it's still possible to enjoy the summer heat and the three autumn weeks in September before the short autumn turns into a long, long winter. The August sunlight seems to last forever. The days are 20 hours long and the vegetables and flowers grow to humongous sizes, reflecting the amount of sunshine they absorb. Giant pumpkins and sunflowers look like papier mache versions of themselves made for a Hollywood set.

Marilyn Ellner, my friend and traveling companion, and I spent a month in Alaska cruising the Inside Passage, making stops in Ketchikan, Skagway, Juneau and Sitka, a week in Denali National Park, a week on the Kenai and Katmai Peninsulas, and a week further inland.

On the boat trip along the Alaska coast, it rained non-stop. I asked a crew member if he thought it would rain the next day and without hesitation he said, "Yes." I found out later that we weren't going to the Tongass National Forest, but to the Tongass National *Rain* Forest, which they somehow neglected to mention when we booked our destination.

Our first inland stop was with Elderhostel (an excellent educational tour company for travelers over 50) at Denali National Park. To protect the environment, private cars are forbidden in Denali and park buses are used instead.

Marilyn and I sat at separate windows on the bus to get a greater variety of photos. Marilyn, who was a photographer, was busily shooting while I was absorbing the scenery, using my camera only occasionally. Through my long telephoto lens, which I used instead of binoculars, I could see that the dots moving on the adjacent mountain were actually dall sheep and mountain goats grazing. An occasional eagle gliding and swooping overhead seemed to gently cover the life on the mountain with a protective blanket even though, potential predator that it was, could, in a moment's notice, destroy this bucolic scene.

After a while, I realized I no longer heard the birds singing. Instead there was an eerie silence emanating from the outside. Then intermittent screeching, as if one bird or animal was shouting to another, sending out a warning. Sure enough, I saw it *was* a warning. A wolf was coming! He sauntered down the mountain and took his place in front of our bus. Like the king of the neighborhood he was, he proceeded to stroll down the road at his own pace leading the parade of buses behind him.

Inside the bus we had a drama of our own. Marilyn, a photographer who will do almost anything to get her shot, was hanging out an open window in the back. I was holding her by the seat of her pants to keep her from falling out or being pushed out the window by a German man who was also aggressive about *his* picture taking.

The park rangers we encountered were a fount of knowledge about the park, but couldn't, or rather wouldn't answer the following questions they swore people asked:

"Who locks the animals up at night?"

"Who feeds the animals?"

"Who mows the grass?"

Before leaving the park, Marilyn and I were eager to see Denali Mountain up close and fly over it. Formerly called Mt. McKinley, at 20,320 feet, it is the tallest mountain in North America. It is usually socked in the clouds two out of every three days. But we were in luck; the day we were there it was sunny.

The pilot's plane of choice was a single-engine Cessna, the same plane my friend Eli owned. I had flown with Eli many times, but for

Marilyn it was a first, and she was scared to go up in a small plane. I lured her inside with the promise of all the marvelous pictures she could take and convinced her that not only was it exciting, it was safe.

The snow glistened in the sun as we swooped in and out of the mountain crags, holding our breath, in complete awe of the majesty of the mountain. When we landed, our stomachs were still up in the air. The mountain was still bathed in sunlight, and I was able to get a good photo of it. As I was preparing to shoot the mountain again, a cloud came from one side, another on the other side, and in an instant covered it like a heavy scarf on two sides of a child's face. That was the end of picture-taking; the mountain was enveloped by clouds for the next three days! But we were lucky enough to see it, to get up close, to say hello, to take pictures, and almost touch it.

The train ride from Denali National Park to Anchorage was unique. Not only were the seats comfortable, the toilets clean and the windows washed, but we had the best guides: high school boys and girls. They had summer jobs on the trains and were in love with their home state. They had a great deal of information and proudly taught us what they knew. Looking out the window, I saw small villages reminding me of the Long Island Levittown-type houses sitting on top of one another. Their backyards were facing the train tracks and in each yard, instead of a car, was parked a small bush plane—the usual means of transportation. Eighty five per cent of Alaska was inaccessible by road due to the deep winter snow and the plane was the vehicle of choice.

The ride was a perfect ending to a fabulous week in Denali. We experienced something that wasn't an everyday sight: the mountain glowing in a colorful, breathtaking sunset showing itself in all its beauty, seemingly making up for all the days it was in hiding. We rode off into the sunset—a true Hollywood ending.

For the second lap of our trip we needed to fly from Anchorage to the Kenai Peninsula to meet our group. At the local airport where we were to pick up a small plane for our short flight, the man behind the counter took one look at Marilyn's luggage and shook his head.

"Lady, there's no room on this plane for your luggage and you'll have to pay $10 for every pound over."

Marilyn began to cry. She still had two large suitcases with her. I have neglected to mention the incident at Newark Airport at the beginning of our trip, which was Marilyn's first since she was widowed. Shall I say she over-packed? She packed for the cruise and the land trip and thought she needed five suitcases worth of clothes. I roared with laughter when I saw her sitting at the airport surrounded by all her "necessities."

She was defensive, "I need it all."

After our boat trip, not only did she send home all the clothes she wore and didn't wear on the cruise, but an additional 50 pounds of stuff she now saw she could do without. However, she still had two large suitcases, a shoulder bag, a personal bag, and her two cameras as we tried to get on this small plane in Anchorage.

I pleaded with the man to let us on with no extra charge. I told him the story of the suitcases, and he too laughed. Luckily, there were no other passengers on our flight which made more room for us and easier for him not to charge her.

When we got to Kenai, the people welcomed us. We were billeted in homes, courtesy of the locals. Marilyn and I stayed in the home of the mayor and his daughter who were warm and outgoing and delighted to see us. Because the inhabitants of Kenai were isolated from the mainland and the world at large, the mayor and his daughter initiated the idea of Elderhostel trips, ours being the first.

The people on Kenai welcomed not only tourists, but also looked forward to the fishing boats that docked, bringing sailors from other countries. The marriages that resulted were warmly welcomed and the outsiders immediately became family. It was also great for diversifying the gene pool. Many of their young people went to Anchorage for a college education and found themselves missing their community. Those that didn't adjust to big city living either went back home and/or abused alcohol.

Each home had its own private sauna, which of course we were invited to share. I had no hang-ups about nudity, but it did feel a bit strange starting a conversation with virtual strangers with clothes on and ending the conversation sitting in the sauna, sweating away, naked. After the first time, however, it felt perfectly natural and became a routine we looked forward to.

Our week was spent sharing our hosts' daily lives as well as having lectures about Alaska, going on field trips and seeing bears first hand. Bears eat garbage and love to forage in garbage cans. After people dump their garbage, the bears wait for the vans and trucks to leave before throwing the garbage can lids off and start eating their delicious meal. But if the vehicles don't leave, the bears don't show up. I wanted to watch the bears and our hosts had a way of tricking them.

We would go in two trucks. One truck would dump the garbage and drive away; the other truck with me and Marilyn in it, would remain to watch the feast. The bears would think all the humans had gone.

It worked. When the sound of the first truck was far away, the bears came to the site to feast. They were brown grizzlies and big! They lifted the lid, rolled the can, dumped the garbage to the ground and ate and ate and ate. It may not be as healthy or as natural but it is certainly easier than trying to catch salmon.

The day before we were scheduled to leave Kenai, we spent a warm sunny day on a fishing boat in the surrounding seas watching the fishermen hauling Dungeness crabs. Crabs were caught like lobsters in wooden traps. The fishermen hoisted the traps filled with crabs as they dropped empty traps into the water for the next catch. While watching the fisherman at work, we passed small rocky islands of horned puffins and sea lions sunning themselves on the rocks. Some rocks had a white covering of *guana* (bird droppings) used for making fertilizer, another large industry in Alaska.

That night, our last on the peninsula, the group had a farewell party. Instead of our usual marvelous salmon dinners, we feasted on the delicious freshly-caught crabs.

Marilyn arranged a free trip for us to go on a seaplane to the Katmai Peninsula to watch bears catch salmon. In return, she promised to give the pictures to the owner to use for marketing purposes. People buying this trip got a money back guarantee, "If you don't see bears, you don't pay." This guarantee was not hard for locals to fulfill. They knew the bears' habitat: where and when and even which bears would appear.

We flew in a small seaplane with two other passengers and landed on Brooks Lake near a small stream that emptied into it. We spotted a bear waiting for salmon at the stream. None appeared.

Once we landed on the lake, I got out of the plane and, with great difficulty, maneuvered to stand on a narrow ledge on the outside of the plane. There was no room to move; behind me was the side of the plane and in front of me was the lake.

Camera in hand, I watched the bear jump into the lake. I thought, "What fun." And then I realized he was swimming directly toward me without stopping. Instead, my heart stopped. He was so close that using my telephoto lens I couldn't get his entire head into the frame of the one picture I was able to get! Luckily, the flash didn't go off to spook him. I plastered myself against the side of the plane to make myself as flat as possible. He kept swimming toward me. I ignored Marilyn's cries of, "Shoot it, shoot it," coming from the other side of the plane. I knew she couldn't see that I might be in danger. He swam up close, real close, looked me directly in the face, then made an abrupt full turn and swam back toward shore. I started to breathe again and felt lucky I was not mistaken for a salmon lunch.

The next few days were spent in Anchorage, a frontier city with a population of about 250,000, sandwiched between the Chugach Mountains and Glacier Bay. The people were different from those in the "lower 48," (as the Alaskans would say.) They were pioneers, settlers, and to me resembled Israelis and Australians in the sense that they were building new countries and new states. They were informal, friendly, open and warm, and yet gruff and a bit taciturn as well.

We spent time in Anchorage walking through town, spending an entire day in the Anchorage Museum. Not only did they have indigenous art, but a big show by Chihuly, a marvelous, innovative well-known glass sculptor from the Seattle area. At the museum I bought a beautiful Inuit stone sculpture of a seal, smoothed down and small enough to be held in the palm of my hand.

Outside the museum, in a small shop selling indigenous art, I bought a fabulous addition to my large mask collection: a small mask of a shaman with one eye closed, looking both inside and outside his world. It was a gem! It's my smallest mask and my favorite.

Being there on a Friday night, we were able to attend services at a Chabad House, an orthodox Jewish outreach sect, joining about 20 people. I admired these young Chabad rabbis and their wives, who were sent to all parts of the world by their revered Rabbi Schneerson of Brooklyn to bring Judaism to the wandering Jew—wandering both around the world and wandering in his/her Jewish or not-so-Jewish journey.

In our meanderings we came to the site of the opening ceremonies of the Iditarod, the huge annual sled-dog race in Alaska which incorporates the original dog-sled trail used to deliver mail in the olden days. Mushers and dog teams set out from Wasilla, the official starting place of the Iditarod, racing 1,049 miles to Nome, through magnificent starkly beautiful yet treacherous country of rugged mountains, pristine tundra and expansive sea ice.

The last lap of our trip was Fairbanks, an inland city that got us close but not quite to the Arctic Circle. Second best to being at the finish line of the Iditarod in Nome, was visiting the home of Mary Shields, an Iditarod musher. We met her magnificent Siberian huskies and Alaskan malamutes, and were shown how they were trained and cared for. Along with preparing for the Iditarod, this was Mary's life's work. Mary Shields was the first woman to finish the Iditarod in 1974 and Libby Riddles was the first woman to win the Iditarod in 1985.

We took a trip out of Fairbanks to a remote area, miles from the city to a man-made town. Old buildings were salvaged, transported to a site where a quaint shopping mall was created to look like an original pioneer town.

Marilyn and I wandered into a jewelry shop and browsed. The owner was a very attractive young Inupiat woman who spoke perfect English. Next to her shop was a general store/souvenir shop. The minute we walked in I felt at home; I heard the proprietor speaking loudly to a customer in a Brooklyn Jewish accent.

"Hello Brooklyn," I said when it was our turn to be waited on.

"How can you tell?" he asked.

"I heard your accent."

We began talking the usual, "Where in Brooklyn are you from?"

"East Flatbush," he replied

"What street?"

"East 49th Street."

"My husband lived a few blocks from there on East 55th Street," interjected Marilyn. "Did you go to Tilden High School?"

"Yes, I graduated in 1955."

"So did my husband"

"Did you go to PS 208?"

"Yes."

"You were in the same grade as my husband!" screamed Marilyn incredulously. "Did you know Jerry Ellner?"

He smiled, not believing what he was hearing, nodded his head vigorously and shouted "Yes!"

"Did you know Jerry's friends — Marvin, Norman and Joe?"

He exclaimed, "We were childhood friends and all hung out together!"

We laughed in disbelief and after reminiscing about the olden days like *mishpuchah* (relatives) he asked, "Did you see my wife's jewelry in the shop next door?"

I nodded yes.

I bought something I didn't need, left the store and headed back to our hired car. I was in a daze and pinched myself.

Was it true? Here I was, near the Arctic Circle in Alaska, and instead of being in an igloo eating blubber with an Inupiat family, I was in a souvenir shop owned by a nice Jewish boy from Brooklyn who was a boyhood friend of Marilyn's husband.

34
Representing the Older Women's League Before Congress

How Social Security Discriminates Against Women

(Testimony by Evelyn Goodman before the Retirement Income Subcommittee of the U.S. House of Representatives Select Committee on Aging. Ms. Goodman is a Human Rights Specialist at the White Plains Regional Office.)

Good Morning, Chairman Hughes and distinguished members of the subcommittee. My name is Evelyn Goodman. I am very excited and honored to be able to testify before this subcommittee and to be a part of our nation's legislative process. Thank you for the opportunity.

I appreciate the subcommittee holding a hearing on this very important issue concerning women. I'm here to speak not only on behalf of myself, but for all women in similar situations — women working all our adult lives in and out of the home and now finding ourselves with a retirement income that is almost non-existent, given the nature of the Social Security Law.

I am divorced, was married for 18 years and raised two wonderful children, one of whom was an assistant U.S. attorney in Washington D.C.

I began working at age 15 at a summer job and I worked part-time all through college. My adult working career started at age 20 as a teacher in a day care center for disadvantaged children in Bedford Stuyvesant in Brooklyn, with a salary of $1,800 per year. I moved to the Board of Education where I taught kindergarten and got a higher salary — $2,500 a year.

When I had my children, there was no choice for me about staying home to raise them. How could I give my love, caring and training to other people's children and allow mine to be cared for by a baby-sitter?

But what I did not know then was that each year I was out of the paid work force on child care leave, I was accumulating "zero" years. They would be averaged into my Social Security contributions and would really diminish my benefits in years to come.

When my husband and I were separated, I went back to work out of the home, substitute teaching in the New York City public schools and being a TV producer for an educational program on Channel 31, the New York City public television station.

I taught multihandicapped children, profoundly disabled children and gifted children before I came to the New York State Division of Human Rights, where I am currently assigned to the Westchester Regional Office to investigate cases of discrimination.

Now that I am considering retirement, I began to look into my Social Security benefits. To my consternation, I found that zero averaging was discriminating against women. Women are adversely affected as they are out of the work force on average 11.5 years compared to men's 1.3 years.

I have found out from the Social Security Administration that my monthly social security benefits will be $450 a month due to the 14 zeros I collected being wife, homemaker and mother and working in traditionally low paying women's work. $450 a month in New York City in 1990 cannot even rent you a single room with a kitchen burner and a toilet in the hall in a slum tenement building.

A man with average male earnings compared to my female earnings and with no zero years would be receiving $704 a month, or more than one and a half times my benefits. This difference in benefits amounts to $3,048 a year or $36,576 over 12 years.

My life has been devoted to public service. All my jobs have been giving to society in what I believe is an important and meaningful way. Society is telling me it didn't value my work then and still doesn't now.

If I may compare my situation to that of First Lady Barbara Bush. Mrs. Bush also spent her lifetime giving to society, by raising a family and doing volunteer work and helping her husband's career. When some students at Wellesley criticized Mrs. Bush for not being a good role model, the public, the media and policymakers for both parties came to her defense. Most everyone was quick to provide value to her contributions to society.

But in fact, we live in a society that only recognizes her contributions through rhetoric and not through economic security. Mrs. Bush's retirement income is totally dependent on her husband's contributions. She, too, could be one man away from poverty.

I helped organize the recent Northeast Regional Conference for the Older Women's League in New York City. At this conference, a key staff person of Senator Daniel Patrick Moynihan stated that it would be possible for Sen. Moynihan, who chairs the Social Security Subcommittee of the Senate Finance Committee, to hold a hearing on women and Social Security this year. We intend to make sure that this hearing comes to pass.

The devaluation of women's work and contributions will continue unless Congress can provide the leadership to make changes. I implore Congress to provide that leadership.

Thank you.

EVELYN GOODMAN studied at Brooklyn College and Columbia University, served as a teacher, TV interviewer and producer, arbitrator, Special Assistant to Commissioner Kramarsky, 1978-82, and Human Rights Specialist in White Plains. She is retiring August 1.

35
Addendum to Testimony

After I gave my testimony, one of the congressmen on the committee, a Republican from Iowa, came over to talk to me: "Thank you, Ms. Goodman. Your testimony was very helpful to me personally. My wife and I are going to have a baby and we had been strongly considering she stay home and care for the baby. Now, after your testimony, we are going to have to rethink our decision."

The same congressman immediately introduced a bill to eliminate a mere three accumulated zeros from the calculation in determining Social Security benefits for women. The bill did not pass; the ostensible reason was there was no money in the budget. There never is for bills benefitting women.

36
The Book Party

Jody's mother-in-law, Wynona, decided to throw a party to celebrate the three books the three men in the family had published: Fred's book, written about his time in Germany when the wall was coming down; his brother Saul's book on philosophy, and his father's book on Educational Psychology.

The party was called for 2:00 PM at a restaurant in Inwood, a neighborhood in northern Manhattan about an hour away from my apartment on the Upper West Side. I left home at 1:00PM, allowing myself lots of time, and walked to the 86th St train station for the ride up to 231st St.

I got on the train without looking, assuming it was the # 1, the only train I have ever seen run on that track. I sat down, deep in thought, wondering how it would be spending time at a family party. It reminded me of the old chestnut, 'If you think you're realized, try going home and spending Thanksgiving weekend with your family!' I looked up from my thoughts and was sure I was on the wrong train. I hurriedly got out of the car, crossed Broadway to the downtown side and took a train back to 96th St where I could get another uptown train. (I wasn't on the wrong train; I only thought I was.) After all that train-changing, I finally got to the 96th St station. As I was getting on the train, I looked up to see Phil in front of me getting on the same train. Since I didn't want to spend the next 40 minutes hearing him talk about himself, I pretended not to see him. But he saw me and waved hello with his cane. I reluctantly sat down next to him and the conversation began. After about 10 minutes of talking about his pending hip replacement surgery, he changed the subject to a mutual friend. Phil conjectured she might be gay and then said, "Why shouldn't she be? After all, men don't treat women very well."

Smiling, I said with tongue in cheek: "Now you tell me?"

When we finally got off at 231st St, he couldn't walk up the hill. Without touching him, I steered him to the restaurant. I felt sorry for him, something I never thought I could do. He couldn't walk, he couldn't hear because of all the years of rock and roll music blaring in his ears, and he seemed old. Old and sick.

We finally got to the restaurant and walked in together, talking animatedly like old friends. I was sure people were in shock. Wynona did say something to that effect. It was good that Jody saw we could be friendly and sociable when the occasion arose. And maybe it was because she couldn't handle us being together that she gave us alternate year invitations on Thanksgiving. She once told me she didn't believe I forgave him. Maybe now she could see that I had.

When it was time to leave, Phil invited me to go with him, since we lived 10 blocks from each other and were going in the same direction. I accepted and we left together for everyone to see.

I smiled to myself. The Universe had me take a very circuitous route to place me on the same train as Phil. Coincidence? I don't believe in it. Synchronicity? A euphemism for coincidence. Destiny? Maybe. Another test? For sure.

Have I really forgiven him? I don't know for sure. But I was getting there.

37

The Road Gets Shorter

I was at the ashram on a two-week retreat. During a morning study session we divided ourselves into small groups for an afternoon session. I had wanted to go to a group in another building but found myself assigned to this particular group. It seemed like random placement.

There were six of us sitting in a circle, and we went around introducing ourselves, saying where we were from. After introducing myself as a New Yorker, the next person, a woman of about 50, said, in a German accent, "I have been in the U.S. for 30 years and come from Berlin." Looking at me, she added, "a city very much like New York."

"No," I said without emotion, "New York has Jews."

After the session was over, I went to the shoe room to get my shoes. She followed me and with tears in her eyes, looked into mine and said, "I know the words are trite. I have no words to say except 'I am sorry. I am so sorry for what happened.'"

I, too, teared up, took her hand and we fell into an embrace. She was crying. "You are the first person who has ever accepted my apology."

We talked and talked. She told me that ever since she was a young girl she had never agreed with Hitler and left Germany as soon as she could. At one point, I told her what the sage Rabbi Abraham Joshua Heschel said, "Some are guilty, but we are all responsible."

We decided that we both, as one, would donate money to the Children's House so they could buy *asanas* (prayer rugs) for the children. Together we went up for *darshan* with the Guru and offered her our gift. She smiled and gave us her blessings by bopping us on the head and gently stroking our faces with her wand of peacock feathers, acknowledging the profound experience of mutual understanding we had just lovingly shared. I walked, no, floated back to my seat on a cloud of joy.

The woman and I exchanged addresses and phone numbers, but we never saw each other again.

38
My Three Bat Mitzvahs

In 2003, my synagogue, the Society for the Advancement of Judaism (SAJ), announced it was offering a year-long Bat Mitzvah program inspired by Rabbi Joy Levitt, wife of the rabbi, Michael Strassfeld, for women who were never given the opportunity to become a Bat Mitzvah when they were 12 or 13. Until Rabbi Mordechai Kaplan, the founder of the Reconstructionist movement and first rabbi at the SAJ, conducted a first-ever Bat Mitzvah ceremony for his daughter in 1922, this rite of passage in Judaism was reserved for boys only. For the first time in the history of Judaism, a girl was permitted the honor of reading from the Torah and was considered a participant in the congregation. However, the Bat Mitzvah ceremony did not become a widespread practice in Judaism until the second half of the 20th century.

I immediately said yes to the opportunity of becoming a Bat Mitzvah. In order for me to do so, I, who knew nothing, *nada, nienety, gurnisht*, of the Hebrew alphabet, pronunciation, trope, cantillation or language, took on the challenge of learning to read and chant Torah.

The day before the big event I practiced walking down the aisle of the synagogue to the *bimah* and reading from the Torah. As I got close to the *bimah* where the Torah lay open, I felt a wave of the energy of the *Shechinah* (the divine energy) flowing out of the scroll and into me. I started to shake and asked Cantor Lizzie for a moment to compose myself before I started to read. It was thrilling reading from the Torah for the very first time! The letters of the words were jumping off the scroll directly into my mouth. I was actually reading the words! Not memorized, not transliterated, but reading!

This profound experience will always be with me, and I was able to share it with the congregation.

On the day of the Bat Mitzvah, 12 days before my 75th birthday, I read my *parsha* (Torah portion) with confidence, without hesitation or errors. After all the other women read their Torah portions, the rabbi did something quite unusual. While we were singing a rousing *niggun* (a devotional melody without words), the Torah scroll was unfurled and wrapped around the entire congregation. The *Shechinah* filled the sanctuary. It was palpable! It was inspiring! It was incredible!

After the Bat Mitzvah service was over, two congregants who did not believe in God, approached me. They told me that because of what I'd shared about the letters coming to life, they too had had that experience when being wrapped in the Torah. Another woman said that because my words came from my heart, they opened her heart in a way she had never experienced before.

And so, the miracle of the *Shechinah* flows ever wider and wider.

In appreciation for what I received, I wrote letters to Rabbis Levitt and Strassfeld:

June 10, 2003
Dear Joy,
As the Kotske Rebbe said, "God dwells wherever you let Him in."
Last Saturday, at the adult Bat Mitzvah celebration, you welcomed God with your inspiration and love.
You brought out the best in all of us, and together with Michael and Lizzie, deeply touched everyone and gave us an unforgettable experience of God.
Thank you.
Love,
Evelyn

June 10, 2003

Dear Michael,

Discussion is great, but we at the S.A.J, during our Bat Mitzvah ceremony, experienced *God's blessings.*

Reading from the Torah with God's blessings we blessed ourselves, blessed each other, and with the Torah being wrapped around us, blessed the entire congregation.

Nobody at the SAJ that morning will ever be the same.

Thank you, Michael, for your leadership and inspiration.

Love,

Evelyn

I threw myself a big party celebrating my becoming a Bat Mitzvah on my 75th birthday.

In 2008, the SAJ offered a *B'nai* Mitzvah class, this time to include men who either never had a Bar Mitzvah, or who wanted a more meaningful experience as an adult. I enrolled. When I told my grandchildren I was going to become a Bat Mitzvah for the second time, they asked, "If you did the Bat Mitzvah thing five years ago, why are you doing it again?" I explained that Bat Mitzvah to me meant the beginning, not the end of study and it was a privilege to be invited to partake of the ritual again. I had another reason as well. The book being studied this time was *"Back to the Sources,"* edited by Barry Holtz, a book I had wanted to study in depth. I needed a teacher like Michael to help me unpack this scholarly work.

In doing so, a remarkable thing happened.

I had read stories about the Berditchever Rebbe and always wanted to learn more about what he actually said and taught. I have the two-volume book the Rebbe wrote, *"Kedushah Levi,"* sitting on my bookshelf. I treasure them, open them and caress the pages, yearning to understand the teachings.

There was a chapter on Hasidism in Holtz's book, and I gravitated to it. To my delight I found it was a homily taught by the

Rebbe. The Rebbe saying about Passover: "The parting of the Red Sea, that was no miracle. Changing the course of nature is no great surprise. But the change that took place in the hearts and minds of the Israelites—that was truly miraculous. Cowardly and fearful slave masses gained courage to prepare for their liberation. They attained an inner liberation that preceded the physical deliverance on Passover. Herein lies the greater miracle."

I got goose bumps! It was amazing! I have repeatedly said on my spiritual journey, "The parting of the Red Sea, that was no miracle. Me forgiving my ex-husband, *that* was a miracle!" Here I was, a descendent of the Rebbe, 225 years later, using the exact words he used back then in the 18th century. It was as if I were sitting on his knee, hearing his voice teaching me.

It was 2014, and I announced I was studying for my third Bat Mitzvah. A third Bat Mitzvah? Again, my grandchildren disdainfully asked, "Why?" This time I answered in typical Jewish fashion, "Why not?" I then seriously told them—again—"Torah study is a lifetime endeavor and I want to delve deeply into its mysteries." When Romemu, the synagogue I was now attending, offered their first adult B'*nai* Mitzvah class, how could I resist? It would be a two-year in-depth study of Torah, reading *midrash* (interpretations), writing our own *midrashim*, learning Hebrew and chanting Torah, with a community of fellow seekers, given by Rabbi Jessica and Sam Klein. This was much more of a challenge both in depth and breadth than my prior one-year experiences.

I was most grateful to Rabbi Diane Kohler-Esses, the Educational Director at Romemu, for allowing me the privilege of partaking of this tradition for the third time. The class started with six men and more than 20 women, and ended with one man and seven women. Monday night was study night—three hours of back-to-back Hebrew and Torah study. I even took an additional Hebrew class Sunday mornings from the superb teacher Jeremy Rosenshine.

Jessica Kate-Meyer, who was then the Assistant Rabbi of Romemu, was in charge. She was the mother hen of us chicks. She nurtured us, encouraged us, lovingly prodded us, taught us Hebrew, trope, answered foolish questions and taught us with love and patience. Jessica was inspiring. Along with the responsibility of "us," she was studying for her ordination as a Rabbi. Except for the last two classes before her examination, she did not miss a single Monday night class. During this time, we celebrated two weddings, a conversion, Jessica's ordination, and became a close community.

I learned a great deal during these two years. What I came away with was an understanding of the relevance of the Bible and how it has been interpreted and reinterpreted through the ages (*midrash*). *Midrash* made the people in the Bible come alive and relevant to me in the 21st century. When our brilliant teacher Sam Klein said, "Art is *midrash*," his words struck a deep chord. Of course. I then realized, "If art is *midrash*, then life is *midrash*!"

We wrote many *midrashim* and were asked to choose one to illustrate in a three-hour art session. I chose to write about Abraham and the Sacrifice of Isaac.

Midrash on the *Akeidah*—the Sacrifice of Isaac
Abraham took the wood for the burnt offering and put it on his son Isaac. He himself took the firestone and the knife, and the two walked off together.   Genesis 22:6

The Lord spoke to Moses...this is the ritual of the sin offering: the sin offering should be slaughtered before the Lord. At the spot where the burnt offering is slaughtered; it is most holy.
                                                                Leviticus 6:27

Isaac was bewildered. His father, Abraham, was preoccupied and walking as if in a trance, preparing the wood, knife and firestone in a very determined way. Isaac ruminated, "What's happening? What is he doing? Why? Why is there no sacrifice?" And then it hit him, "*I am going to be his sacrifice!*" The enormity of the situation overwhelmed him.

Isaac trembled with fear and disbelief. "He tells me he loves me. Words. Only words. How could he even think of sacrificing me? Why didn't he plead with God to save his only child, his beloved child of his old age? He pleaded for the people of Sodom, for my cousin Lot. Am I not more precious to him?"

> Here I venture to speak to my Lord.
> I who am but dust and ashes.
>
> Genesis 18:27

Isaac: Maybe I can talk him out of this murderous act. 'I'm no fool, Papa, I see there is no animal sacrifice.' (Hesitating) Am I to be the sacrifice?

Abraham: I love you, Isaac, my son. More than my own life. I would gladly lay down my life to spare yours, but I am acting on God's command. I cannot disobey. My heart is breaking.

Isaac: What manner of God do you worship? I can't believe it is His will that you kill me. He doesn't want you to kill me. I think God is testing you to see *if* you will kill me. Please pass the test! Don't kill me!

(*Abraham* does not answer.)

Isaac: If you kill me you will destroy your seed for future generations and turn your chance for posterity into ashes. Your God promised He would make unto you a great nation. I don't believe God means to break His promise to you.

(*Abraham* remains silent)

Isaac: (Pleading) Papa, I love you. Please don't do this.

(Abraham picks up the knife and goes toward *Isaac*, who watches in horror as he sees the hand—the hand of his father—holding the knife glistening in the sunlight coming closer and closer toward him to slit his throat.)

Isaac: My heart is broken. Even if God intervenes, I AM ALREADY SACRIFICED.

Evelyn Goodman
Nissan 5775

We were also asked to write a very short *Dvar Torah* (interpretation of our Torah portion). My portion was The Priestly Blessing:

22 The Lord Spoke to Moses:

23 Speak to Ross and his sons: thus shall you bless the people of Israel.

Say to them:

24 The Lord bless you and keep you!

25 The Lord deal kindly and graciously with you.

26 The Lord bestow His favor upon you and grant you peace.

27 Thus they should link My name with the people of Israel, and I will bless them.

Numbers 6:22-27

My *Dvar Torah* was:

We, the children of Israel, don't need the High Priests to give blessings.

We can bless each other.

Some of us may feel unworthy of blessing others or even ourselves. On the other hand, we may feel what Rabbi Levi Yitzhak of Berditchev calls pseudo-piety, when we become filled with self-importance in fulfilling *mitzvot* (a commandment of God.)

To let go of all of these feelings is to become an empty vessel. From that place, God's blessings can flow through us. In this way, we can bless one another, and the Berditchever says, "When we give blessings, we also bless God." This gives God much pleasure and He *sheps nachis*, He *kvells*, like a proud parent.

Bless someone, sometime. It feels great! My blessing this morning is:

Bless the thoughts leaving your mind

Bless your empty mind

Bless the you that is now the empty vessel, the temple of God
Bless the you, a giver of blessings
Bless God, for being God
Shabbat Shalom

A Blessing by Danny Siegel
inspired by Talmud *Berachot*: (for students who study)

May your eyes sparkle with the light of Torah,
And your ears hear the music of its words.
May the space between each letter of the scrolls
Bring warmth and comfort to your soul.
May the syllables draw holiness from your heart,
And may this holiness be gentle and soothing
To the world.
May your study be passionate,
And meanings bear more meanings
Until Life itself arrays itself to you
As a dazzling wedding feast.
And may your conversation,
Even of the commonplace,
Be a blessing to all who listen to your words
And see the Torah glowing on your face.

39
Ashram Moments

In the ashram, any and all holidays were a good time to celebrate. It was Passover and some of us Jewish New York devotees prepared a program to present to the Guru. Despite our protests to the head of the program committee, who happened to be Jewish, we were only given 10 minutes.

The Guru enjoyed our presentation, and when it was all over she smiled and said, "You wandered in the desert for 40 years and you give me only 10 minutes." She was not only showing her pleasure with our presentation, but was also ending any further discussion concerning the viability or length of any future program we wanted to do. We had her permission.

She then playfully pointed to people and asked, "Are *you* Jewish? Are *you* Jewish?" Those of us who were, answered yes; the majority answered no. And then she said, "*I'm* Jewish."

I called out in a loud voice, "When you're in love, Guruji, the whole world is Jewish." She roared with laughter.

The following year, the same New York devotees were doing a program for *Rosh Hashonah*, the Jewish New Year, and needed to borrow the *shofar* (the Ram's horn traditionally blown on the New Year) we had given the Guru as a present the year before. I had the pleasure and honor of presenting it to her and while doing so inadvertently upstaged the actress who was waiting to meet with the Guru.

When I asked Guruji for the *shofar*, she smiled and said, "Yes, you may borrow my *shofar*. But be very careful with it. I have it sitting on my *puja* (altar)."

The respect and love she showed the *shofar* touched me deeply.

My mother, at age 92, died on a Thanksgiving weekend while I was taking an intensive. During the program, which I took lying on my back on the floor due to severe chronic back pain, a huge picture of Babaji's Guru, weighing hundreds of pounds, fell on me. Miraculously, I was not hurt, and it appeared I broke the fall for the other people sitting near me. In the amazement of escaping injury, I jokingly said, "What a way to get the touch!"

My friend Arnie said that in his meditation, he saw my mother hovering over the hall showering us with blessings.

After dinner I went to the temple to pray for my mother's easy transition. The temple was closed. When I told the person in charge that my mother had just died, he allowed me inside. Meditating in the rarefied atmosphere of the temple and saying the mantra lessened my sorrow and, I hoped, helped my mother cross over to a better place.

40
Vienna

The winter of 1990-91 was an exciting time to be in Germany. The wall was crumbling in Berlin, and my first grandchild was born in Bonn. I was overjoyed at the prospect of seeing little Betsy and spending time getting to know her. However, I was still very uncomfortable going to Germany, even though my trip to Heidelberg with my Guru the year before had rid me of the heavy baggage of fear and hate.

After a week, believing that Jody's new family should bond without me, I went on a 12-day journey behind the crumbling Iron Curtain, to Prague, Budapest, Krakow, Vienna, Auschwitz, and back to Bonn.

For some unknown reason, I was disappointed with Budapest and cut my stay by a day, giving me extra time in Vienna. I had made up my mind, because of Vienna's World War II Nazi history, I would hate it. Quite the contrary. Despite my having a landlady who gave off anti-Semitic vibes, buskers who were singing Yiddish and Gypsy songs that made me feel like an artifact—first they kill us off and then they sing our songs, finding a poster in the foyer of Freud's apartment advertising a concert of Leonard Bernstein portraying him stereotypically with an anti-Semitic long crooked nose;, and literally the worst Chinese food in the world, I nevertheless was enchanted by Vienna.

I had a 9x12 map of the city, and I found my location at the bottom. It was a Friday, and I had all day to explore. I wanted to find a synagogue for services, but there was no mention of a synagogue on the map. However, on the very top, 12 inches away, was a street with a church that I thought might have a shul. It was worth a try.

I decided to leisurely wend my way up to the top of the map and said out loud, "God, if you want me to get to services, you'll have to get me there. It's in your hands."

Exploring Vienna was a treat. I walked through markets, went into the beautiful main cathedral, ate delicious *Sacher tortes* and *Linzer tortes* at a *Konditorai* (bakery) and even found one of the apartments Mozart lived in when he was in Vienna. It was there he wrote *"The Magic Flute."* In fact, I was able to buy the last ticket to a performance of *"The Magic Flute"* for the following evening. How thrilling to hear *"The Magic Flute"* performed in Vienna!

I wandered further up the map to the top, found the church and sure enough found a synagogue on the street across from it. There were armed police guarding the street and male congregants on patrol. It hurt my heart to see that 46 years after World War II, Jews still had to be protected going to prayer.

I walked through the door of the shul, which had a turnstile and a man blocking the entrance. I was asked all kinds of questions, like, "Where do I come from" and "Do I belong to a shul?" After answering to his satisfaction, I asked the man who was questioning me, "What time are services?"

"Six o'clock," he replied.

I looked down at my watch. It was five minutes to six!

41
How the Hunter College Campus Schools Were Saved

New York City in the 1970s was in turmoil. Not only was the city on the verge of bankruptcy, it was also a time of tumultuous activity regarding education. Parents were clamoring for more of a voice in the educational system: wanting changes in the curriculum, and some wanting complete community control of education with an end to the central Board of Education.

There were also misguided demands to abolish the special schools, like Bronx Science, Stuyvesant, Boy's High and the Hunter College Campus Schools, calling them all-white and elitist.

Fortunately, Hunter Elementary School had extended its boundaries into Harlem and was not all white. The original boundaries for admission to the campus schools were 59th Street to 96th Street and from the East River to Central Park. Later, the West Side was included, and in the late 1960s, the boundaries extended north to Harlem. We were an integrated school.

The Hunter College Campus Schools, among the oldest in the United States, were founded in 1869 as a Girls' Normal School for Teacher Training. The schools are now under the auspices of Hunter College and the Board of Higher Education, paid for by appropriations by the New York State Legislature. In 1964, men were admitted to the college; the high school remained all-girls.

Historically, the City Colleges of New York were tuition-free and open to all residents with a high school diploma who passed a qualifying exam. Now there was a vociferous demand for a drastic change in the enrollment process. It was for Open Enrollment, with no qualifying academic entrance exam!

Both my children were students at the campus schools—Jody in the high school and Nicky in the elementary school, which made me a Hunter parent. During all this, we Hunter parents were very quiet. We told Jacqueline Wexler, President of Hunter College, we didn't wish to interfere in pedagogical or administrative policies. All we wanted was an assurance that she would support the continued existence of the campus schools. She called the elementary and high schools, "Islands of Excellence," and assured us she would keep her word.

In 1970, Open Enrollment became the official policy for the City Colleges. And Jacqueline Wexler announced she was abolishing the campus schools! To accommodate the influx of new students, President Wexler needed the physical space we occupied at the college campus on Lexington Avenue, and the funds that were allocated for us. We were in her way.

She wasted no time throwing the high school girls off campus, housing them in a commercial building, 466 Lexington Avenue, near 46th St, in the center of one of the busiest neighborhoods in the city, three blocks from Grand Central Station and across the street from a porn shop. Not exactly the place for the 12-year-old girls in Jody's seventh-grade class.

The elementary school was moved under the 59th St bridge into an old, decrepit, abandoned building owned by an order of Dominican nuns. When they decided to sell the building, rather than making the necessary educational improvements, they shunted us to a vacant building on Sutton Place that formerly housed the UN School.

In early 1972, President Wexler announced that due to Gov. Rockefeller's anticipated cut to Hunter College's budget by six million dollars, she would be forced to abolish the campus schools. Although closing the schools was only a threat and not a *fait accompli*, she told the teachers to look for other work. Our only hope of staying alive was to convince the governor and the New York State Legislature to provide the funds we needed and to find a new location for the schools.

Jacqueline Wexler, an ex-nun married to a Jew, apparently learned very little about Jews. She didn't know how tenaciously Jewish parents would fight for their children's right to a quality education. She underestimated us. We would pull every political string to fight her.

We went to work.

A committee of three was formed. The President of The Parents' Association, Ruth Widder, an East Side resident, had a summer home in Montauk and knew Perry Durea, the Republican Speaker of the Assembly, who represented Montauk. I, Vice President of the Parents' Association, a political activist from the West Side, worked on the mayoral campaign of Al Blumenthal, minority leader of the Assembly and my Democratic Assemblyman, and knew him well. And then there was Bob Kagan, the lawyer and father of Elena Kagan, a student in the high school who would grow up to become a Supreme Court Justice.

We mobilized the school. We met with Percy Sutton, Borough President of Manhattan, Sandy Gorolik, President of the City Council and Robert Kibbie, Chancellor of the Board of Higher Education. Bob Kagan and I met with our West Side legislators and Ted Weiss, our friend and city council member. Ruth met with her East Side legislators, Republican Assemblyman Roy Goodman, and her Democratic Senator, Harrison Golden, a Hunter Elementary School graduate. I met with Fred Orenstein, West Side Democratic Senator, whom I knew from our Brooklyn College days together.

The parent body made phone calls, wrote letters, signed petitions, sent telegrams to the Governor, and met with their city and state legislators. We contacted not only our representatives in Albany, but Long Island and upstate legislators as well. A group of parents went to Albany to lobby the same legislators one-on-one for their support. We got press coverage from *The Daily News*, *The New York Post* and *The New York Times*.

The 1973 New York State budget was scheduled for a vote o March 24th, 1972. On March 23rd, we held a large rally in front of Gov. Rockefeller's office and home on 53rd St and 5th Ave. We had a permit to block traffic and, armed with placards, saying "SOS, Save Our Schools," hundreds of students, teachers and parents took up the rallying cry loudly and passionately.

I was told by someone very high up in the Board of Ed, who was a candidate for the position of president of the college after Jacqueline Wexler left, that the 1973 New York State budget was held up and would not pass until there was a line item in the budget for the campus schools. I found it hard to believe, but my source assured me it was true.

All the while, we were looking for adequate space for the schools and after years of searching found something we thought was perfect—a vacant public school on Park Ave and 94th St. It was built on the border of two neighborhoods—the posh Upper East Side and East Harlem, pulling students from both neighborhoods. It was thought to be the perfect way to integrate the school. But it didn't work. The residents of Park Ave were not happy since some of the kids attending the school were not on their best behavior. Eventually, the experiment was considered a failure, and the school was closed. The building, on the site of a former armory, was sitting empty. When the neighborhood residents were told of the possibility of Hunter becoming the tenant in the vacant school, they embraced the idea enthusiastically.

Matching the school building with Hunter seemed simple enough, but it wasn't. We hit a wall of political bureaucracy. The school and the land were under the auspices of the Board of Ed; the campus schools were under the auspices of the Board of Higher Ed. The Board of Ed was not relinquishing the land and building to the Board of Higher Ed that easily.

Two huge behemoth organizations locking horns.

After much wrangling, infighting and pulling political strings, the two boards came to an agreement. Meanwhile, the girls in Jody's class of Hunter '76 spent their entire six years at the high school in an office building and graduated from a makeshift, unacceptable physical facility.

Renovations were made, and the elementary and high schools were eventually reunited and moved into their permanent quarters in 1977. It took seven years, but we used the system to beat the system!

The schools were saved!

42
Getting the Boys into Hunter High

Saving the schools was a job half-done. The battle was not over; now we had to get the boys into the high school. Through the years, Hunter Elementary School parents murmured about getting boys into Hunter High School, but no one did anything about it. Now the time was right to approach the administration. Having worked together to save the schools, we parents and administration felt like family. It was a perfect storm.

Since the high school started in seventh grade, the admissions test was given in sixth grade, and Nicky was entering sixth grade, I decided to do something in time for boys to be eligible to take the test, which was given only once.

I was a single mom making very little money producing a TV show for the city station and couldn't afford private school tuition. Public school was not an option; it was dangerous and hardly a place for serious education. Because special high schools, like Boy's High or Bronx Science, started in ninth grade, they were ruled out since there was no middle school for Hunter boys.

As Vice President of the Parents' Association, I contacted the New York Civil Liberties Union, my Councilman Ted Weiss, as well as Dr. Bernard Miller, Coordinator of the Campus Schools about the issue. Dr. Miller said the Administration was against having the boys at Hunter, but he personally would not oppose us. He gave me his informal blessings and said, "Evelyn, do what you have to do."

We formed a committee of three sixth-grade parents—Rita Katz, Joyce Hyman and myself—to spearhead the fight. We called an open meeting of Elementary School parents at my house and at that meeting decided to hire Eleanor Jackson Piel, the attorney who got the girls into the all-boys Stuyvesant High School the year before. We collected money and got to work.

We had lots of opposition, not only from the Administration. The angry voices in the community-at-large, were still calling for the abolition of all special schools, labeling them all-white and elitist.

The Administration objected because there were no bathrooms for boys, there were no athletic teams for boys, uniforms would have to be provided, and there was no money for such changes. Internally, some of the faculty were against the idea. The male teachers welcomed the idea with open arms; not all the female teachers did.

And interestingly, many of the high school girls themselves objected. They had fears the teachers might neglect them in favor of the boys and they would somehow be overshadowed. Being aware of boys in the classroom changed the atmosphere and they couldn't be themselves. Some worried they didn't want to appear smarter than the boys and wouldn't make a good impression. Others felt girls would start to dress up for the boys and that boys were a distraction. The focus would not be on education. Some of the older girls objected; maybe because they were rueful that they wouldn't be around to enjoy the new energy boys would bring to the classroom.

I understood the girls' concerns but told them they would have to face studying with boys in college. Confronting the situation now would make them stronger later on. And it might even be fun.

The Alumni Association was also against the idea of boys. A "Hunter Girl" was very special (and indeed she was). They wanted to keep it that way.

We had some salient arguments on our side. Hunter had extended its northern border into Harlem some years back, and we were an integrated school. Most importantly, we had legal grounds. The boys would have no place to go for seventh and eighth grade; the public high schools started in ninth grade. They were being discriminated against as boys. They did not have access to equal quality public education as did the girls.

We filed a lawsuit, which was scheduled before a judge in late February, 1974 (Hyman vs. Board of Higher Education).

Jacqueline Wexler had learned by now, having lost the fight to abolish the Campus Schools, that we parents were determined. Instead of a court battle, we got a surprise victory. A few days before Valentine's Day, she called a press conference and said, "The girls will get a Valentine's Day present. Boys will be admitted to the High School."

There was enormous pressure on the 22 boys who applied for admission. On the day of the test, walking down Park Avenue to the back entrance of the High School, Nicky was confronted by the press. They were out in full, thinking only of getting a story and not what this day meant to these 11-year-old boys. The boys all passed the test and were now able to take advantage of the marvelous educational opportunity, which had been so long in coming.

Nicky, Jody, and I were sitting at the dinner table relishing our victory, when Jody said to me, "Mom, parents have been talking for years about getting the boys into the High School. But somehow I knew it would be you." It was a cherished compliment and the sweetest frosting on the victory cake.

It wasn't easy for the boys. Through the years there was attrition while the above-mentioned obstacles sorted themselves out.

Nicky graduated with seven boys and 188 girls in 1980, in the first class of boys at Hunter!

Watching Charlie Rose on TV recently, I discovered that Lin Manuel-Miranda, creator of the Broadway super-hit *"Hamilton,"* was one of the boys who benefited from going to Hunter. He said he felt he won the lottery getting into Hunter, and it had changed his life. Hearing this, I felt I played a tiny part in the creation of *"Hamilton."*

I wrote Lin Manuel telling him the Hunter saga. This was his reply:

Evelyn,
Thank you kindly for your thoughtful card. Although my currently hectic schedule doesn't allow me to grant your request at this time, please accept my sincerest gratitude for everything you did for all of your 'boys.'
Siempre,
Lin Manuel

I read this letter while the TV was on and to my delight, there was Lin Manuel on television. I wrote to him telling him of this "coincidence." He replied, "The world can always use a bit more magic and serendipity."

43
Cuba

Cuba was a very difficult place to visit before President Obama eased the restrictions on relations between the two countries. The only legal way for an American tourist to get to Cuba was to go with an educational or religious group. Yetta and I joined a "religious" tour given in 2009 by the Jewish Community Center (JCC) of Manhattan. The Havana Jewish community was on our itinerary, as were architectural walking tours of Havana, browsing the markets, visiting artists in their homes, baseball games, music, and dancing.

I informed Batya, the group leader, I needed a wheelchair at the airport. When she said the Cuban authorities could not comply with my request, I insisted. "I must have a wheelchair. I can't move in the airport without one." My firm request upset her. "Evelyn, you know you'll have to *walk* in Havana." I assured her I could walk, but I couldn't pull my suitcase in the airport due to my sciatica and torn rotator cuff. I got the wheelchair.

We brought the Jewish community medical supplies such as aspirin, Tylenol, antibiotics, and first aid items, as well as slightly worn clothing. Among other things, I brought a size nine flowery lilac bikini for some teenage girl to enjoy, knowing ruefully I could surely never fit into it again. The community shared these supplies with all their neighbors—Jews and non-Jews alike.

Before getting off the bus after a busy first day of visiting schools, going on an architectural tour of Havana, and visiting a Jewish cemetery, Batya briefed us on the evening's activities. After dinner, the tour would provide us with partners to go dancing if we wished. Our group was intergenerational, with ages ranging from 26 all the way up to Yetta and me, age 79. Batya asked, "Who would like to go dancing?"

Yetta and I, along with some of the younger women, eagerly raised our hands. The second night was more of the same.

On the third day of our trip, as I was getting off the bus, looking forward to another evening of dancing, Batya took me aside. She laughed as she said, "Evelyn, I have a confession to make. When you asked for a wheelchair at the airport, I was very concerned. I was sure I had an invalid on my hands, someone who couldn't walk. And here you are going dancing every night."

I then told her what my dance partner of the previous night said to me as he took me in his arms and our bodies began undulating to the sensual rhythms of the rhumba. He looked down at me, smiled approvingly and said, "You've done this before!"

44
Between Two Passovers

Passover: a time for celebrating freedom, freedom from our own inner Egypt, freeing ourselves from the prisons we have created for ourselves, the prisons with the cruelest and most unbending of guards—ourselves.

Ruminating on my quest for freedom ,I thought back to Passover 1989 in Germany, when my journey began in earnest. I, who said I could never forgive the Germans and who would never, ever go to Germany, found myself at a retreat with my Guru, in of all countries, Germany. I instinctively felt, with her protection, this was my chance to begin my arduous and scary journey to freedom.

I came to Germany to try to forgive the Germans, and I had the life-changing realization that the same feelings I had for them I also had for my ex-husband. I knew then I had the impossible task of forgiving him in order to be free. Through the years, I had been letting go of the *Schmutz* (dirt) little by little, forgiving him incrementally, overcoming enormous resistance. I had also been saying, "The parting of the Red Sea, that was no miracle. Me forgiving my ex-husband—*that* was the miracle."

While I was studying for my second Bat Mitzvah, I came upon remarkable teachings about Passover by Rebbi Levi Yitzhak of Berditchev. I was astonished, and still am, at what he said, "The parting of the Red Sea was no miracle." He went on to say that changing the hearts and minds of the Israelites from a slave mentality to one of fearlessness, to want to go out from Egypt into the unknown, in search of freedom, having the courage to inform the Egyptians beforehand, and for the people to have an inner liberation, that was a miracle! And that is the miracle of Passover!

During Thanksgiving 2013 at Jody's house, I knew my freedom was in sight. But there was a last piece of "stuff" I still clung to and had to deal with—the huge challenge of the apartment. Phil and I each owned half of the Riverside Drive apartment I was living in, an apartment I had insisted we move into. Before the move, when Jody was four and a half and Nicky was just a six-month old baby, Phil had been on a 10-day escapade to Europe with a married woman. Soon after, when our case was in Divorce Court, Phil pleaded with the judge to have us evicted so he could occupy it. When I asked him "How could you even think of throwing us out of our home?" he snarled through his teeth. "I always told you to take care of yourself."

Shortly thereafter, the Riverside Drive building went co-op. Just as we bought the land in Amagansett with *my* pension money, (which meant resigning my permanent New York City teacher's license and guaranteed security) so, at my insistence, we took out a mortgage and bought the apartment. For all his arrogance, he was timid and couldn't make up his mind or take adult risks.

It was *my* work, *my* energy and *my* money that enabled Phil to now own half of a valuable apartment on Riverside Drive. Upon my death I didn't want him enjoying the money he would receive from the fruits of my labor, particularly since when we were in divorce court he'd petitioned the judge to evict me and the children. It was one thing to forgive him and yet another thing to reward him.

Since we owned the apartment as "tenants in common," neither of us could sell without the other's permission. His wish to evict me could only come true when I died. And so, my will stated that Jody was not to sell the apartment until her father was 92. (I really wanted to say "upon his death," but I didn't think she would react kindly.) But now, with the gentle prodding of my therapist, I had finally come to the point where I no longer cared how he would lavish luxury on himself with the money I'd worked so hard for. I had decided to give myself the precious gift of freedom—unshackling myself from him and breathing free.

Recently I changed my will. Jody was now able to sell the apartment upon my death with no conditions! My journey of forgiveness had ended. I was free!

Unbelievable though it was, I believe my journey of forgiveness had ended. It could not have happened without my tenacious love of life, a remarkable therapist, and a loving God who is with me always.

While writing this I became aware of another miracle. The active part of my freedom journey had begun in Germany on Passover 1989 and ended in Washington 2013 on Passover.

And it only took 25 years!

45
A Healing Meditation

I was sitting for meditation when Phil came to mind. It made me sad and angry remembering all the pain he created for the people who loved him the most.

I went into meditation. Phil became an enormous octopus with three long tentacles and a huge eye in the middle. The creature radiated pure pain. Rather than being soft or round, the tentacles were large, sharp arrows shooting out pain. Then Jody, Nick, and I each became a tentacle. Phil was the eye in the middle and from this eye, like a madman, he was frantically radiating pain to each of us.

We were writhing in this excruciating agony when suddenly again, from out of nowhere, I shouted, "God, please forgive him."

46
India

I love retreats: being away from the phone, mail, TV, newspapers, computer, and the many other distractions of everyday life. Being able to turn inward and spend uninterrupted quality time on my *sadhana* (spiritual journey), eating good food, being in the company of other seekers, and spending time with the Guru or learned Jewish teachers is a bit of heaven.

Whether it be four week-long visits to the ashram in India, or summers in the beautiful Catskill mountains, or Jewish retreats in Connecticut and the Hudson Valley, retreats recharge, refresh and enable me to deal with whatever comes up in this complicated affair called life, with more equanimity.

I was in India. We were immersed in a two-day workshop called "The Mantra, The Guru and You Are One." As I started to say the mantra *Om Namah Shivaya* (I honor my Inner Self, the God that is inside me), I went into meditation. In the meditation, I started to say the mantra and felt my tongue getting bigger and thicker until it became a strong rope. I began swinging on it; the Guru joined me. We began swinging together, laughing and having fun, enjoying the freedom. She took me for a wild exciting ride through the universe. We were having a great time. Then we both sat down on swings in a playground. As we were swinging, we were kicking what appeared to be pebbles under our feet as we touched the ground. Only they weren't pebbles. They were planets!

During another meditation session, I found myself in a rowboat going down a small slow-moving river. It was quiet. The quiet was quiet. A standing oarsman was rowing the boat as we slowly glided down the river past small wooden houses, like the ones found in the *shtetlach* (small towns) of Eastern Europe in the 18th and 19th centuries. I felt as if I was in *Siddha Loka*, (the heavenly realm where *Siddhas, Tzadikkim* and Saints are purported go when they leave their earthly bodies.) The river, like the River Styx in Greek mythology, seemed to be the road to this special place.

We sailed in this stillness for a long while and passed many houses, finally stopping at a long pier. Still in the silence, the boat pulled up. I climbed out of the boat and walked to the end of the pier to a small wooden house. I got to the door and it opened. On the other side stood the Berditchever Rebbe! When he saw me, he jumped in the air, touched his heel with one hand and thrust the other above his head as he leapt high in a dance of ecstatic joy.

There was a flash of blinding light, and I came out of meditation.

47
Thoughts on Meditation

Please don't think every meditation is like this. There were many, many days, weeks and months of dry meditations with my mind racing a mile a minute. The mind's job is to think streams of thoughts that never stop. Thoughts keep us from going beyond the mind to a place where we can experience the bliss of who we really are. We can taste that through meditation, the key that opens the door.

Sometimes I would make a deal with my mind. "Okay mind. You have 10 minutes. Do your thing; then it's my turn." And many times it worked. After the mind raced through thought after thought I would have a quiet, relatively thought-free meditation. Fighting the mind never works; it is much too powerful.

48
My Crowning Achievement—Clara N.

You don't have to be young and a beauty queen to get hit on by a man.

Clara N. was a plain, 50-ish, ordinary-looking woman who came to my office with a complaint of sexual harassment. She worked for a very large corporation in Westchester as a secretary in an administrative pool for a group of male executives and was filing a complaint naming one of these men.

When an alleged improper sexual incident occurs, there are usually no witnesses, only "he said - she said." How to discover the truth? The Division of Human Rights had two avenues to follow: did the complainant tell a credible person at the time of the alleged act and/or did she keep a diary?

One of Clara's bosses in the pool made ongoing, verbal, sexual advances which she tried her best to ignore. When her husband died, the situation worsened.

"Can I fix your plumbing?"

"Do you need work on your electrical system now that you have no man around the house?" And other such crude, gauche, inappropriate remarks.

She was very uncomfortable, continued to say "no," and tried to make light of the situation. One lunchtime, Clara told her bosses she was going home to do some important chores and though she didn't expect to, she might be a little late. Her boss volunteered to go with her. She said, "No," but he followed her in his car anyway. When they got to her driveway and got out of their respective cars, she didn't invite him in. He said he was thirsty. "Couldn't you just give me a glass of water?" She felt threatened, but also felt he was her boss, and she couldn't be rude. He came in and it began.

He told her he wanted to go up to the bedroom; if not, he would have her fired. She was very frightened. She needed the job even more now that she was widowed and had to support herself. Still mourning the death of her husband of many years, she was alone and vulnerable. Feeling she had no options, she succumbed.

She said nothing until many months later when she was told she was selected to become this man's personal secretary. She couldn't tolerate the situation any longer and went to the company's Human Resources Department. They didn't believe her story. This man was very well thought of in the company and his wife was the private secretary to an executive in top management.

This forced Clara to come to the Division for help.

During my investigation, I discovered that Clara had kept a diary all her life and had written it all down. Then I learned that two former secretaries of the respondent had left because of sexual harassment, but they refused to come forward. I also learned his ex-wife would not allow him to visit their two daughters. I wondered why. In his response to the complaint, the respondent said something strange. He gratuitously said that he played with children in his neighborhood and they all loved him. It felt creepy.

I could have found probable cause and have the case sent up to the Administrative Law Judge, where it would have languished for one to two years due to the Division's large backlog. I wanted to settle the case; I wanted Clara to have closure. The company aimed their biggest legal guns at me and fired a barrage of questions.

"If what Clara said really happened, why did she send him postcards while she was on vacation?"

"She wanted to make nice; she still felt the threat of losing her job," I replied.

"Why was she friendly toward him?"

Not to have been friendly would have been conspicuous; he was her boss, after all.

I tried to settle the case, but to no avail. After many months of investigation and attempts at a settlement, we were at a standstill. Without consulting me, Clara went to the top feminist lawyer in New York City who told her the case was worth her $28,000 yearly salary. No more. Clara and I both agreed the case was worth much more. I had been asking $100,000; the company was offering $5,000. During negotiations, they raised it to $10,000; I didn't budge.

Clara wanted to go to the local newspapers, but I convinced her to give me a little more time. I told the respondent's lawyer Clara wanted to go public, but I had advised her to wait. Negotiations were still going nowhere, and it was then I called a conference for the following Monday with the respondent, his lawyer, and Clara.

Monday morning came and with it the shocking news that during the weekend the respondent had taken a gun and shot himself in the mouth.

We settled for $56,000; two years' salary!

There would be a non-disclosure and a no-fault clause in the agreement. That didn't mean nothing happened and they had done nothing wrong, only that they wouldn't admit it. These were usual stipulations in settlement agreements.

Clara's employment was terminated, but in any case, she didn't want her job back. She was given a recommendation for employment elsewhere. Clara knew it would be very difficult to get another job at her age and decided to do something she always wanted to do. She would paint full-time! She rented a small reasonably-priced house in the New Mexico desert and would live on the $56,000.

She spent the next two years happily and productively as a painter and invited me to visit. Unfortunately, her happiness was short-lived; she developed cancer and died a short while later. However, thanks to the settlement money, Clara was able to fulfill her dream of becoming a painter, enjoying the last two years of her life.

In 1990, the year I retired, I negotiated $250,000 for complainants and went out in a blaze of glory!

49
Meeting Bat-El

HIGH SCHOOL
Meeting Bat-El
by Evelyn Goodman

On my last visit to Israel in 2008, I told myself that on my next trip I wanted to do service for Israel, meet the student I was sponsoring through NACOEJ, and go to Petra. I have just returned from that trip.

I found a marvelous, rewarding work-study program sponsored by Hadassah called WIN (Winter in Netanya) where volunteers come for a month or two to Israel and do things like teach English to Ethiopian teen-agers. I can't call it work; it was a privilege.

I was assigned to an Orthodox live-in high school for Ethiopian boys, and helped them with conversational English so they could pass a test after high school and be prepared for life.

These boys were an inspiration! They were so happy to be in Israel, proud to be citizens of the country, and were eager to go into the army to start their new lives after high school.

They were like sponges – gobbling up the time we spent together. This is what teaching is all about – instant gratification for both student and teacher.

I was talking with one boy named Birku and he was telling me about his plans for the future. He was filled with eagerness, optimism and ambition. It is kids like this who will make Israel proud.

I asked him if he had been to Gondar. He said he and his family were there for six years waiting to go to Israel. I asked him if he had ever heard of NACOEJ. His face lit up into this beautiful smile, he jumped out of his chair and his hands flew to the ceiling, and he shouted, "NACOEJ SAVED MY LIFE". He was so excited, and when I told him I was sponsoring a female student through high school, he thanked me profusely – as if I needed thanks."

Bat-El and Evelyn. Photo: Leah Barkai

And then my cell phone rang. It was Leah, a representative of NACOEJ in Israel, telling me that arrangements were made for me to visit my student in Rehovot. I gave the phone to Birku for him to tell Leah what he said about NACOEJ. I sat there filled with wonderment, as Rabbi Abraham Joshua Heschel would say – in radical amazement.

Two days later I went to Rehovot to meet Bat-El, my student at the ORT secular day school. It was 3 pm on Sunday, after school had finished. Bat-El was at the gate, with a friend, waiting for me. We hugged and kissed and went with her teacher up to her 7th grade classroom.

She shyly asked me about my family. I brought pictures of them along with postcards of New York, "I Love NY" T-shirts, and "I Love NY" teddy bears for her and her sister.

She made me a beautiful present – a large ceramic hamsa with both our names written on the front to hang on the wall. She must have spent many hours on this plaque and I was very moved.

She told me her father made aliyah when he was 21, met her mother in Israel, married, and when Bat-El was father remarried, had another child and is now divorced. He works in a spice factory and makes a home for the three of them.

I told her my story. My parents came from Ukraine at age 18, met in Bucharest on their way to America, and were married. They had no money and no family and I am a first-generation American. We have something in common as Jews – our families had to leave their country to come to a strange land and start a new life. But thank G-d, Jews now have Israel to come to.

I taught her two Yiddish words, "Shayneh Punim" (pretty face), and asked for an Amharic word. She offered one in Hebrew.

Her hobbies are dancing, looking at photos of her mom, reading weekly Torah portions with her father, reading books, and talking to her cousins. She wants to be a banker or work in the high-tech field.

I brought bubbles, as ice-breakers, and we giggled as we took turns blowing. Of course, we took pictures.

After a while, she said she had to go and she and her friend left, but not before I told her that I would sponsor her through high school, if she wished. We said our goodbyes and Leah drove my friend and me (I, too, brought a friend along) to the train station and our ride back to Netanya.

By the way, I did get to Petra and walked all the way down. ■

50
The Divine Messenger

Although Greenwich Village is one of my favorite places to walk in New York, I hadn't been there in a long time. But one balmy, spring evening, I found myself on Christopher Street to hear my friend David, a fellow meditator, do a standup comedy gig.

I was early and had time to browse in the shop windows on the block. I came upon a Tibetan store, and since I was traveling to Tibet later that week, I walked in. The woman behind the counter was Tibetan and we began to talk. She told me she left Tibet in 1959 when the Chinese Communists invaded and now lived in New York with her two nephews. Her husband, however, lived in Nepal.

I asked if I could do anything for her. She hesitated for a moment, and then said,

"Could you take a letter to my sister who still lives in Tibet?"

I asked, worriedly, "Will I put your sister in harm's way?"

I wasn't concerned about my safety. I felt as an American citizen I was above harm. She assured me her sister would be safe and told me to get the letter from her husband, Wangchuk, in Nepal, where he owned a rug factory.

The first thing I did when I got to Nepal was to call him, but I couldn't make contact immediately. Luckily, the Chinese government was playing head games with Americans and was indiscriminately bumping them from flights to Tibet. My traveling companion, Marilyn, and I were marooned in Nepal for four days. Well, hardly marooned. We were put up gratis by our tour operator at the Yak & Yeti Hotel, the finest luxury hotel in Kathmandu. Built more than 100 years ago as a magnificent palace, it had beautiful emerald green gardens and antique fountains. Four days gave us time to explore Kathmandu and the neighboring villages, take a single engine plane ride over the Himalayas and Mt. Everest, cross a river atop an elephant during a rainstorm in a national park, and finally make contact with Wangchuk. We met him at the hotel cafe. Over lunch, he gave me the letter for his sister-in-law in Tibet, blessed me and blessed my journey. From there he took us to his factory where he proudly showed us around. It was a living shrine to the Dalai Lama who had instructed Wangchuk to open a factory to give work to his fellow Tibetans under humane conditions. The factory was spacious, light and clean and even had child care facilities. The weavers were women of all ages. Babies were beside their mothers at the loom, while the older children were in a separate supervised playroom. It hadn't been easy to get into Tibet; the Chinese were still playing games. Because they were only allowing groups of Americans in, our tour manager arranged for Marilyn and me to be paired with other Americans traveling in twos and we became a temporary group for entry purposes only. Once we crossed the border, a young Tibetan woman named Tenzen was assigned to be our guide. I presumed our guide would be Tibetan and was very surprised when Tenzen told us guides were usually Chinese. This was one of the ways the Chinese were systematically destroying the Tibetan culture. I drew her into conversation, wondering if I could trust her with my clandestine mission. Before I left the U.S. I had read about Dharamsala, India, where the Dalai Lama lived in exile, along with the children who were carried across the border in 1959 when the occupation began. Tenzen told me that, as a child, she was in Dharamsala with the Dalai Lama, and now that she was grown, he had sent her home to help her people. This eased my mind a bit, but I still didn't fully trust her. I needed to know more. "How did the children live?" I asked. "Where did you live?"

"The children's quarters were in a long narrow house built just for us." And then, Tenzen said in a low, teary voice, "I miss him so much." I said something about the Dalai Lama being in her heart and she could always find him there. Tenzen nodded, smiled and by the expression on her face, conveyed a deep love. Her longing touched me and made me feel I *could* trust her. "I need to get in touch with a friend who lives in Llasa," I said. "Could you help me?"

She nodded her head, "Yes." "I have a letter. Here is the name and address. Could we possibly find her?" I handed Tenzen the letter. Tenzen looked at the name and shrieked with amazement. "I know this woman, Tashi. She's the mother of my best friend!" Tenzen then told me she had been scheduled to be out of the country on another trip at this time, but for no apparent reason she had been assigned to us!

"Could this be the reason I was reassigned?" Tenzen exclaimed. I smiled to myself. I believed our meeting was destined. Last year I had been forced to postpone my trip to Tibet when I fell and broke my foot on a ship going down the Yangtze River, headed for The Three Gorges. The Chinese government was going to flood this beautiful natural wonder to build a dam, and I wanted to see it before it disappeared.

To me, being in Tibet at this time was no coincidence.

The next day, Tenzen arranged for us to meet Tashi for lunch. The restaurant was plain and simple. Not so Tashi. She was beautiful and elegant, wore diamond-studded earrings, looking very much like an upper middle class woman. She apologized for being late and for her husband's absence. She had walked a long way from her home to the restaurant, and her husband couldn't walk that far. She spoke English very well and after some small talk, I gave Tashi the letter from Wangchuk. She opened it and tears poured down her face. Enclosed were pictures of her two boys, now grown, whom she hadn't seen since they left Llasa as children. I couldn't hold back my tears. I told her that in 1939, during World War II in Europe, Jewish parents had put their children on trains to England (the *Kindertransport*) in order to save them from the Nazis, not knowing if they would ever see them again. Tashi did the same in Tibet in 1959 when she sent her two boys to Dharamsala.

We had a light lunch, during which time she invited me and Marilyn to her home for dinner the next evening. We eagerly accepted. Fortunately, logistics were easy, since our guide was very much in the loop.

Tashi had a small wooden house, and as we walked toward it, I couldn't help but notice the many Chinese flags flying from the neighboring houses. The Chinese government was doing a great job of destroying a culture. They were forcing Chinese people to relocate to Tibet, making Tibetans a minority in their own country. Also, they were stripping the monasteries of their treasures, exporting precious, ancient Buddhist artifacts to Nepal for sale. They were destroying the monks as well, the human treasures of the monasteries. Tashi and her husband, Namdak, welcomed us into their home in the traditional way: placing a beautiful white silk shawl around each of us. The interior was simple with a few small rooms, not the kind of house one would expect from someone who wore diamond earrings. Namdak was most charming, and I quickly found out why he couldn't make the trek to the restaurant. He had been a monk living in a monastery. The Chinese tortured and beat him and his fellow monks, forcing them to leave the monastery, take wives and live a worldly life. He survived the ordeal, but was left badly crippled.

Tashi invited us to sit in the living room and served us warm tea with milk. It was delicious and reminded me of the hot milk-sugar-hot water mixture I drank as a child. I later found out it was the yak-butter tea I had definitely decided beforehand I would never drink! In the room was a large private altar with a picture of Tashi and Namdak with the Dalai Lama. I was taken both with their personal relationship with His Holiness and by their audacity. Having pictures of the Dalai Lama was illegal and their act of defiance could have had serious repercussions.

Tashi was distressed, telling us of the boys' situation in the United States. The American government didn't believe they were Tibetan refugees and needed proof of citizenship. She gave me pictures of the boys as small children in front of the Potala Monastery as proof they were indeed raised in Tibet. I assured Tashi that the pictures would get to her sister in New York via her brother, Wangchuk, in Nepal. I told her I would do everything I could, including going to the Department of Immigration to vouch for her children's citizenship.

Our conversation brought to mind my visit to the Potala Monastery the day before. It was the largest monastery in Tibet. The Chinese hadn't closed it, but were using it as a showplace for tourists. It was on top of a steep hill, and today I would call the climb arduous. Upon entering, we were ushered into the room where the Dalai Lama gave blessings to his followers. It was dimly lit; the darkness gave the room an other-worldly quality. The shabby furnishings looked like the remnants of the lost way of life that had been. I imagined the Dalai Lama sitting on the divan, greeting his followers, who were eagerly waiting on line for their *darshan* with this holy man.

As I approached his seat, I felt a strong energy pouring out. I put my hand on the divan and felt the energy going through me as if the Dalai Lama were actually present and blessing me with his loving touch. It was palpable. My mind returned to the room as I heard Tashi inviting us to dinner at her nephew's restaurant the following evening. What a joy to be spontaneous and unencumbered by a tour schedule!

The next day was full. First, Marilyn and I visited the local market. Asia was a 24-hour bazaar of exquisite exotica. Wherever one turned there was something fascinating to feast one's eyes on. This market was filled with practical everyday necessities, as well as prayer wheels, pendants, clothing, prayer flags, and shawls. Even a non-shopper like me could become an addict. I bought jewelry and a small prayer wheel for myself, and prayer flags as gifts for friends.

Before going to dinner, Tenzen took us to the monastery where her brother lived. It was one of the few remaining active monasteries left. She told me Chinese spies were everywhere, even in the monasteries. We entered a courtyard filled with beautiful shade trees and flowers. Monks were sitting together enjoying the warm weather, the sunshine and the studying. I was enthralled by the way the monks studied scriptures—*chavruta*-style—just like us Jews. Working as partners, each monk took turns explaining their point of view of the text they were studying. Some were sitting, others standing; some were loud and excited, others quiet, all trying to prove their point. The difference between the two cultures was that here, one of the two monks had to win the argument. In Judaism, it was just two people studying, arguing and enlightening each other, going deeper into scripture.

While walking from the monastery to the restaurant, we passed many Chinese soldiers on the street. They were young boys, appearing to be no older than 17 or 18. From the look in their eyes, they seemed like frightened, bewildered children. Tenzen told me, along with soldiers, lonely and homesick, came prostitution, something unheard of in Tibetan society.

The restaurant was a small storefront. Inside were a dozen or so plain wooden tables without table cloths or fancy dishes. They were filled with customers and the sounds of relaxed dinner conversation. The two waiters were busy serving interesting-looking dishes that smelled good. Their nephew, Dolkar, was a wonderful host and served copious quantities of indigenous dishes, including roast yak and vegetables. Tibetans couldn't survive without the yak. They were not only the work animal in the fields, their hides were used for clothing, and they were an important source of food. I was a vegetarian, yet how could I come half-way around the world and not taste yak meat? And of course, how could I insult my host? I tasted it. No, it did not taste like chicken. It was juicy, succulent, and delicious, more like a fatty pot roast. However, I had not eaten meat in fifteen years and just couldn't get it down. I hid it in my napkin.

Dolkar lifted his glass, toasted us and our return to Tibet. I had been to countries controlled by dictators, but this was the first time I had ever been in an occupied country that was being systematically wiped out. I lifted my glass and was about to say, "I'll return when your country is free," but a strong intuition stopped me. A moment later Tenzen pointed to two men at a table near us and whispered, "Those men are spies."

Upon returning to Nepal, I immediately got in touch with Wangchuk and gave him the pictures from Tashi. I reiterated my willingness to help in any way I could with the Department of Immigration. He thanked me again, wished me well and we parted. Marilyn and I had an extra day before our flight home to the US. I had been coughing throughout the trip, and Marilyn insisted I see a doctor before we got on the plane. I reluctantly agreed, thinking I might have walking pneumonia. By this time by just looking at someone I could see the difference between Tibetan and Chinese people. As I sat in the waiting room, I recognized the receptionist was Tibetan. Still savoring the magic of the "coincidences" of the last few days, I began telling her my story. After a few moments she exclaimed, "I know that man. He's my brother, Wangchuk!"

Back in New York, I called the Christopher Street store and was told Mrs. Wangchuk no longer worked there. She had taken the boys and moved to Canada. Five months later, she called me, but I missed her call. I was out of the country, on another adventure.

51
God Sometimes Uses a Plane

When I was planning my trip to Southern Africa, my friend Fredy told me her sister-in-law's family lived in Johannesburg. She talked about giving me their address, but never did.

On my way home from a fascinating trip to Botswana, Namibia, Zambia, the Seychelles, Zimbabwe, and South Africa, I took a flight from Johannesburg back to New York. After take-off, I went to the back and center of the plane to find three empty seats to stretch out on. A man with a yarmulke had the same idea. There were only five empty seats and we decided to take turns. However, instead of sleeping, we introduced ourselves and began talking. We talked about South Africa. He said that although he was very happy apartheid was over, and had no complaints against the corrupt government—"After all, all people in power become corrupt"—he wanted to leave the country. The crime rate was very high and it was difficult to live with crime on an everyday basis. He was urging his children to leave. He would stay; he felt he was too old to start a new life.

He told me he was going to his nephew's Bar Mitzvah, being held in a Conservative synagogue in Westchester.

"Do you belong to a synagogue?" he asked.

"Yes, it's a Conservative/Reconstructionist shul."

"Women go to the *bima*?" (podium)

"Yes."

"They wear a *tallis*?"

"Yes."

"I can't get used to that idea. Women don't belong on the *bima*."

"Why not? Think about it. Why shouldn't I be able to get as close to my beloved God as you?"

"Because it says so in the Bible."

"That's because it was written by men."

"No, by God."

"I believe it was written by men inspired by God."

"My rabbi says 'no.'"

"And mine says 'yes.' A different interpretation doesn't make one more kosher than the other. It's the 20th century, and times are changing. Judaism is changing and becoming more inclusive. Women want to express their yearning for God the same way men do."

"I will be so uncomfortable at the Bar Mitzvah seeing women on the *bima* wearing a prayer shawl."

"Please understand our simple love for God. It is pure. It is in our hearts waiting to be expressed."

He seemed to be touched by my sincerity. We finally fell asleep for a few hours without taking turns. I gave him the three seats.

The Monday after the Bar Mitzvah weekend Fredy called me. She was all excited. She told me the man I spoke to on the plane was her sister-in-law's brother and that he was the man whose address she meant to give me. She couldn't thank me enough. Apparently, he had a wonderful time at the Bar Mitzvah and was able to accept the differences that before our talk stood in the way of his truly celebrating his nephew's coming of age as a participant in Jewish life and worship.

And Sometimes Uses A Phone

I pay my credit card bills by phone and more often than not, the phone is answered by a person from a country on the other side of the world. By their accents, I can usually tell where they're from, and a conversation ensues.

One day I got someone from India.

"Where are you from in India?" I asked.

"How can you tell I'm from India?"

"I can recognize the accent. I've been there four times."

He was delighted. "I'm from Bombay."

"I've been to Bombay."

"Oh?"

"I go to an ashram 60 kilometers from Bombay. In Ganeshpuri, to Guruji's ashram. Have you heard of it?"

"Yes, I go there too," he said excitedly. "But I haven't been there in a long time."

I then told him Guruji was there right now. "You can go to see her. She'll be there for a few more weeks."

"I'd like to, but I can't." He sounded dejected. "Because I smoke."

"That's okay. You're allowed to smoke."

"I am?" He asked incredulously.

"Yes, as long as you don't smoke in the ashram."

"I didn't know that." I could hear the smile on his face.

"I will go this weekend," he said gratefully. "Thank you. Thank you."

52
Thanksgiving 2014

I thought sharing my time with Phil on Thanksgiving would be the end of the machinations of who comes when and where and that from now on celebrations would be straightforward.

Boy, was I wrong. Thanksgiving was approaching and Jody called.

"We have a problem, mom."

What now? I thought.

"Fred's parents can't make Thanksgiving; they have complications. We need to be in New York since Philip is not well enough to travel to Washington." She paused, "I know it's too hard for you to do." She paused again. "How would you feel if we had Thanksgiving at Philip's house?"

I gulped. Phil's house! That would feel weird. His personal life. Seeing how he lives. That's getting much closer than I would like. It could be sticky; it could also be painful. Under the circumstances, what else could I say but, "Yes, it's okay, I can handle it."

His apartment was eight blocks away on West End Avenue. I'd passed the building many times, pointing it out in my head, "That's where Phil lives," but never expecting to actually be inside.

When Jody opened the door and I entered, I was struck by the beauty and spaciousness of the apartment. Large rooms on the 15th floor with a breathtaking corner view of West End Avenue and the river. Much more luxurious than *my* apartment. He lived in such opulence while denying me and the children the paltry $5,000 child support and alimony the court required him to pay. As soon as these thoughts and feelings came up, I put them aside. I was going to have a good time. That was past; it was over. I had given all that up.

I had to go through his study to get to the bathroom and felt like an intruder seeing his papers, photographs, books, clothes, and other personal items. Thankfully, I only had to use the bathroom once during the entire evening.

I looked at the art on the walls and was drawn to a painting by a South American painter. Although it was dark and somber, with dark blues and black, it had a light emanating from it that seemed mysterious and spiritual.

I asked Phil about another painting, "You wouldn't want to know about that." I presumed it had to do with Shelly, or Michelle as she was now called.

Phil was an excellent cook, which meant he had a well-stocked kitchen with beautiful dishes and serving bowls. He helped Jody cook; that was his pleasure. With two good cooks in the kitchen, the food was delicious, and the conversation free-flowing, pleasant and mundane: politics, theater, college and of course his health among the topics.

I looked at Phil and saw a sick man, a man I once loved and shared a life with, dying of cancer, and I felt sorry for him. I also mourned a life that might have been had all my childhood dreams come true.

The time passed easily; I had an enjoyable evening with my family. I really *did* forgive him. It seems I had passed another test.

53
Krakow and Auschwitz

Krakow and Auschwitz, the last leg of my 1991 trip, were the hardest.

Although I had been to Dachau, the concentration camp outside Munich, I knew I had to go to the most infamous of all the death camps, Auschwitz, where 1.1 million Jews were murdered. I needed to stand on the platform where Dr. Mengele, the *Malach Hamoves* (the Angel of Death as he was called in Yiddish) decided whether you were or weren't on the line leading directly to extermination.

I had to see it, smell it, feel it in my bones, in my *neshama* (soul) to immerse myself in it, to mourn, to say *Kaddish* and to give thanks that I was a Jew lucky enough to have had parents who came to America.

I spent my first day sightseeing in the beautiful, charming Polish city of Krakow. While walking around, I found a small museum that actually had a *Pieta* by Michaelangelo. It was guarded by a *babushka*, an old lady who sat in a chair without moving a muscle. Such a person was given that name because of the scarf she wore on her head. Every room in the almost empty museum had a *babushka*. It was make-work at its best.

In the late afternoon, I went to the former Jewish Quarter. The main synagogue was now a museum, the *cheder* (children's school) a small bookstore, the bakery a souvenir shop, the tailor's shop a restaurant. There were no Jews, only their artifacts. I walked through with a very heavy heart.

Facing the plaza was a *shtiebel* (small *shul*) that was still in use. And since it was Friday, I went back to services after a small supper. I didn't have much of an appetite.

The synagogue was small and dark with rickety stairs leading up to the women's section. There were 10 or 12 people inside, and I was greeted warmly with smiles and handshakes. They were all old and looked like the remnants they were. When I pointed to the women's section, I was surprised when I was given permission to remain downstairs with the men. All the *davening* (praying) was in Hebrew. I was praying next to a very frail old man. His eyes were red, looking as if they were perpetually crying. In his hand he lovingly caressed an old, tattered *siddur* (prayer book) which was falling apart. I realized it too must be a survivor of the camps.

After services I donated money to the synagogue and walked out onto the plaza. Two men started talking to me in Yiddish and very broken English. I sensed they would ask me for money for themselves, which I was happy to give them.

I didn't know which hurt more: being on the grounds where the Jews were murdered or walking among their homes, synagogues, schools, and stores and seeing and hearing only the ghosts of a vibrant people who no longer existed.

The next day on a very cold, wet and dismal morning, I hired a car and driver for the 30-mile trip to Auschwitz. I arrived to find a scene I had not expected. Instead of being a somber, quiet place, I found it filled with distractions. Steven Spielberg was filming *"Schindler's List"* and the crew created the usual bustle and noise of a Hollywood set. Unexpectedly, there were people carrying picket signs. Apparently, an order of Carmelite nuns wanted to build a convent on the site outside the camp and there was opposition to that odious project.

The driver offered to be my guide inside the camp. I politely refused. I most definitely did not want or need a guide.

The place was sanitized: flowers were planted; buildings were freshly painted. In one building were separate exhibitions enclosed in large circular plastic domes. In one dome was a huge pile of suitcases, in another eyeglasses, in another a pile of shoes, in another gold-filled teeth taken from the corpses of the murdered. I somberly walked along and came to a door which led to the lab where Mengele performed his indescribable subhuman experiments on twins. When finished with their bodies, he discarded them, dead or alive, like garbage.

I learned that Mengele's selection site was in Birkenau, a mile away, and I walked there. The train tracks to the camp went through the gate and ended at the infamous arrival platform. I stood on the platform and tears began to flow. Through tears of pain I tried to imagine what it was like spilling out of the stinking excrement-filled, death-filled cattle cars with the guards shouting *raus* (out), dogs barking, being pushed from one place to another, being prodded with clubs and shouts of *schnell* (fast), being forcibly separated from loved ones, and then either being lucky enough to be selected to live, or doomed to be on the line leading to incineration.

The scene was gone, but my tears were not. They would not stop. I stepped off the platform, looked around, and walked in the bitter cold to some of the barracks that were still standing. These wooden barracks originally housed 42 horses and were converted to squeeze in more than 400 people, with three rows of bunks, one on top of another, three people to a bunk. In the barracks, people had scratched their names and dates on the walls and on the bunks.

Many villages had been destroyed to build Auschwitz, and now there was nothing remaining but a few barracks and the crematorium. As crazy as it sounds, being in Auschwitz, I couldn't believe it ever existed! Everywhere, as far as I could see, were miles and miles of desolation. Here I was, standing in the bitter cold, wearing warm pants, a sweater, a hooded coat, gloves, a shawl and boots, and I was freezing. There was no way anyone could have survived these brutal temperatures, barefoot, wearing the rags the inmates wore. I was shivering. How did they survive?

As I was standing there shaking with the cold, it seemed as if God answered me. "You think *this* is cold? I'll show you cold." From out of nowhere, snow began to fall with the biggest snowflakes I had ever seen in my life. I stood there, growing colder and colder as the wind swirled snowflakes around me. After about five minutes the snow stopped as abruptly as it had started.

The tears froze on my face as I slowly walked toward Crematorium 1 and Crematorium 2. I walked into 1.

Facing me were two ovens. It was then I lost it.

All my emotions let loose. My crying and my inner silent sobs broke into angry words. I began hysterically screaming, "God, where were you? Where were you?"

When I calmed down, I said *kaddish* (the prayer for the dead) for all the Jews who were stripped of their humanness and slaughtered like animals in this place, no one remembering the moment of their massacre.

I smelled the hate. I tasted the hate. It entered every pore of my being.

I had to wash myself clean and somehow move through the grief.

I spent the evening with a young couple in Krakow who had just met my Guru and were thrilled to see me. They welcomed me into their home, to break bread, to meditate and talk. Although they were the children and grandchildren of non-Jews who lived through this time and were probably anti-Semites, these young people were not.

I needed to be with Christians who did not hate Jews, or me, and who loved the universal God in us all. I was enveloped by this love and it was healing.

54
The End of One Journey

Today, if I hear tourists speaking German on the bus or subway, I no longer cringe but turn to them and start a conversation.

"Where are you from?"

"Germany."

"Yes, but from what city?"

"Berlin."

"I've been to Berlin. I went to Germany four times to visit my family who was there for four years. It's a beautiful country."

I ask where they are staying and how long they've been in New York.

"What have you seen so far?"

"The High Line, the new World Trade Center, and walking through Central Park."

"What else are you going to see?"

"A Broadway show tonight."

I was on the 50th Street crosstown bus one day during such an encounter and I began pointing out the sights. "Radio City Music Hall, Rockefeller Plaza, Rockefeller Center, the skating rink and the site of the Christmas Tree."

I was delighted to show them my city. They were enjoying this spontaneous tour so much that they asked me if I would join them and continue the tour.

I reluctantly said no. Had I not had an appointment I couldn't break, I would have been happy to be their host.

55
The Yale Test

It was May, 2013, Betsy's graduation from Yale, and the entire family, including Phil, went to New Haven for the weekend celebrations. Another test for me, again spending an entire weekend with Phil!

But the stakes got even higher when the powers that be at the Yale accommodations desk, seeing the names Evelyn and Philip Goodman, assumed we were married and assigned us to a suite together. Jody immediately said: "Mom, I'll tell them to change the rooms."

"It's okay," I answered, not really knowing that it would be okay, but willing to try.

Phil and I entered the suite, dropped off our luggage and made awkward small talk about how beautiful and spacious the accommodations were. Fortunately, I thought, there was a large living room separating the two bedrooms.

The entire family had dinner together and then went back on campus to hear a marvelous concert by the Whiffenpoofs, Yale's famous a cappella group, and now that Yale is coed, the women's group Whim 'n Rhythm. The women sang beautifully, but I must confess, to me there is a special quality to the sound of a male chorus that is extraordinary and incomparable.

After planning to meet the next morning at the commencement exercises, everyone retired for the night. Phil and I entered the suite, chose rooms and remarked again on the quality of the accommodations. We decided to have breakfast together and then made for our respective rooms as quickly as was politely possible.

I slept as well as I usually do, considering my sleep apnea and my CPap machine. But I was a very light sleeper who was easily awakened. Phil needed to use the bathroom three times during the night due to his prostate condition, and although he tried to be as quiet as possible, my sleep was disturbed.

I lay in bed thinking: "This is what my life would have been, had we stayed married. Him sick, me well; I would have been his nursemaid." It's one thing caring for a person who has cared for you through the years of a long, loving marriage. Quite another to be caring for someone who has only thought of himself.

Once again, I felt lucky to have escaped.

The next morning I waited for him in the living room while he slowly finished dressing. He moved with difficulty as we walked out of the suite and onto the street. I made sure that although I was being helpful with directing his walking, I didn't get too close to him. I didn't want him to take my arm or even brush against me. He still made my skin crawl. Nobody could tell from my behavior that deep down inside he still disgusted me. However much society overlooked his behavior, to me he was a pervert who liked little girls.

We had a pleasant enough breakfast in a crowded coffee shop on Chapel St and leisurely walked to the quadrangle to find the rest of the clan in time for the graduation exercises. So far so good. I had made it through an overnight with Phil in the same suite and breakfasted together with no strong negativity coming up, only feelings of relief, gratitude and yes, even a little pity.

This graduation for me was especially sweet. I thought about my graduation from Brooklyn College in 1948, Jody's graduation from Yale in 1980, and now Betsy's in 2013. I ruminated, "You've come a long way, baby." It felt good.

After graduation exercises were over we had lunch at Berkeley College, still celebrating and congratulating until it was time to go home. Jody and Fred were staying with Betsy; Fred's parents went their own way.

Ouch, this meant Phil and I would be on the same train to New York for two long, tedious hours, me listening to him talking about himself. Once again, I was stuck.

It could have been a nightmare, but luckily the only empty seats on the train were one behind the other. The conductor said: "Sorry, ma'am, you'll have to separate from your husband," as he showed us to the seats. I smiled at him and whispered: "Thanks. He's my ex-husband."

About halfway home, the train pulled into a station and stopped. We were told there had been an accident ahead and this would be our last stop. There would be no train to New York!

After much difficulty we found a taxi that would take us back to New York and for the next one and a half hours, I was a captive audience. We got as comfortable as possible, even though sitting next to him in the back seat was not comfortable. So much so, I put my purse between us as a buffer. After a few minutes of small talk, I excused myself and pretended to nap. I actually did fall asleep, waking up as we approached the outskirts of the city.

I talked about my last winter's trip to Panama and the thought entered my mind that had I still been married to him, I wouldn't have seen the world. I also knew that had I had a choice, I would have chosen a happy marriage with a much smaller taste of the world. But then again, who knows? I might have been able to have had both.

We talked about Betsy and the family when Phil said, in a comforting voice: "I don't know what it is between Nick and you."

"Neither do I."

"He's not easy to be with, you know." And then he went into a diatribe, complaining about how he'd been neglected and mistreated by Nick and that things were not great between them. I appreciated Phil trying to make me feel better and actually wanted to hear more but our conversation was interrupted by the driver asking for directions to my house.

As I prepared to leave the cab, Phil complimented me. "You look good." I couldn't say "So do you" because he didn't. I just smiled and said "Thanks." I gave him $40, my half of the fare, and bounced out of the cab, knowing I had passed another big test.

Maybe I really did forgive him!

56
Reaching The Promised Land

When Jody told me that Phil had cancer, I was surprised at my reaction. In a strange way I felt sorry for him and didn't wish him ill as I had done a long, long time ago. Some friends in my meditation group said they had not only forgiven their ex-husbands, wives, enemies, etc. but had also blessed them and sent them on their way—and out of their lives. I had come to that miraculous place of being able to forgive even after that ugly, debauched breakup. That was enough. I couldn't bless him! Nor should I have to. And that was fine. Then the Great Miracle happened. Shortly thereafter in *shul* at Romemu, I was saying a *mishebeirach* (prayer for health) for Sydell, my friend with lung cancer, and for Jody, to have strength and wisdom in taking care of her father. And from nowhere a tremendous energy poured down on me, and I realized it was a *mishebeirach* for Phil for his good health. And I actually said, "I wish for you to have the courage and strength to face whatever is in store with equanimity."

Me blessing *him*? I couldn't believe it! Forgiving him was miracle enough! *Dayenu!* (enough) But this was even bigger. I was dazed with the wonderment of it all. I was somewhere but didn't know quite where I was or who I was. I stood there—frozen—and thanked God.

The following Thursday was Thanksgiving, and still in miracle time, I spent the holiday with the family at Phil's apartment. Due to his illness, he wasn't able to travel to Jody's house in Washington D.C. where we usually celebrated Thanksgiving. I was able to enter his personal dwelling place, and I was okay! This could be the end of the story, but it isn't. The following Shabbat, the same *shul*, the same prayer for healing, which again I said for Sydell and my daughter. And again, without thinking, I was showered with blessings for Phil. Only this time, the blessings, like a cosmic download, came into my head and through my lips out loud! *I actually spoke them*! Once again I stood there like a stone statue—frozen, astonished. Had this really happened? I got goose bumps all over my body and the tears flowed. This was the Miracle of Miracles! I was able to actually bless him—without thinking—the words coming through my lips. I was saying a blessing for him! As I was bathing in the sweetness of these blessings, I had the realization that in blessing Phil, *I was the one being blessed*! I savored the sweet moment, smiling. I thanked God—not for being in my life—but for my having the ability to have my heart open to allow God into my life and to work His wonders.

One of the great hasidic Rebbes, the Koske Rebbe, was once asked, "Where does God dwell?" The Rebbe answered, "Wherever you let him in."

There's more.

The next Shabbat, the same prayer, different synagogue. Here, congregants stood and when individually recognized, responded to the request, "Say the name of the person in need of healing." I thought for a moment, stood up, and at my turn, mumbled out loud, "Phil Goodman." I thought it was over, but miracles don't end.

A week later, back at Romemu, when the time came for the healing prayer, I thought consciously and with no prompting, stood up, and said in a full voice, "Phil Goodman." It seemed to be complete. But who knows? Only God knows and She won't tell.

On *Simchat Torah* (the holiday of the Torah) each member of the congregation randomly picks a *pasuk* (a verse of Torah) to study for the year. My *pasuk* was Numbers 33:34 ("And they removed from Jotathab and encamped at Ebroanah"). Quite useless, trivial information, I thought. I asked if I could discard this *pasuk* and choose another, but was encouraged to stay with it, study it, and see what would happen. I then read the entire *parsha* (chapter) which is about the wandering of the Jews in the desert for 40 years. The *parsha* is broken into sections of encampment. Pondering what relationship that ancient trip could possibly have to my life, I went over the timetable of my journey of forgiveness:

1974—Becoming aware of my need and my ability to choose to forgive the Nazis.

1974-1989—Lying, unable to move, at the entrance of the forgiveness road.

1989—The Guru's retreat in Heidelberg, Germany, where I realized the hatred, bitterness and anger I was carrying around for the Nazis was the same pain I was carrying for Phil.

1989-2009—Simultaneously struggling with forgiving the Nazis on a cosmic level and realizing, for the first time, my need to forgive my ex-husband on a personal level, one small step at a time.

Telling Phil I forgave him, but not really meaning it.

Slowly, painfully going forward on both fronts.

Reaching a point where I could hear German tourists speaking German on a city bus without feeling pain in my gut. Initiating talks with them with warmth instead of vitriol.

Meeting Eva Kor, a remarkable woman who survived Auschwitz and the atrocious experiments performed on her and her twin sister by Dr. Mengele. Marveling at her ability to forgive Mengele.

Reluctantly telling Phil I forgive him. This time, meaning it.

2009—Progress manifesting in being friendly and helpful to Phil at a family party.

2012—Breaking the custom of having Phil or me every other year at the family Thanksgiving celebration by inviting him to Washington on my year.

2013—Cordially sharing the same suite all weekend with Phil at Betsy's graduation from Yale.

2014 — Letting go of my long-standing resentment that after my death, he could enjoy the financial fruits of my labor concerning the apartment we jointly owned and changing my will. That was the last piece! And a biggie! Finally, finally letting it all go!

Final freedom!

Complete forgiveness!

I then added up the years of my forgiveness journey: 40 YEARS! Just as in the Bible, it had taken me 40 years to get to the Promised Land—and freedom!

Still, to quote Yogi Berra, "It Ain't Over 'Til It's Over."

In 2015, the doctors gave Phil three days to live, but he hung on for three weeks. In that time even more forgiveness unfolded:

I was able, through Jody, to tell Phil I sent him blessings and prayers.

I was able to say a *misheberach* on three more Shabbat services.

I was at the May Romemu retreat in Connecticut when Phil died. Not only did I say *kaddish* (prayer for the dead) that Shabbat, but I was able to sit by the lake with Ken, a fellow yogi friend and Romemu congregant, and chant the mantra for his easy transition from the planet.

The following Wednesday at noon, Jody called me from Washington. She was sitting *shiva* (a mourning and celebration for the dead) that night. Did I want to come? I did. I jumped on the first train I could and got there by 7:00 PM, in time for the prayer service. At the *shiva*, I was able to share with everyone an aspect of Phil he had lost in his later years and that people were unaware of—his wonderful sense of humor.

I do believe I was given these three extra weeks, perhaps by Phil, perhaps by God, to finally complete my journey.

57
Explaining the Inexplicable

My mind said I would never forgive the Germans, never forgive Phil, never let go of the never. How could I drop the anger, sadness and pain, so raw, so real, so appropriate?

Slowly, ever so slowly, I found my heart was surprising my mind. My heart was being awakened to the idea it could say "no" to my mind and become free of its clutches. I was allowing the heart to function without the encumbrances of the mind. Imperceptibly, the mind changed its attitude because this new experience, surprisingly, felt good. Strange, but good.

Something inside me, my *neshama* (my soul) opened to the idea that in order for me to be free from the pain, I had to let go! A new idea! I hadn't realized until then that letting go was necessary in order to live! I probably would have gone through life carrying this burden feeling oh-so-self-righteous and victimized.

My mind became open to a Higher Power to help with this enormous task. I *knew* I couldn't have gone down this path alone and come as far as I had. First the blindness, then the awareness and the glimmerings of another way to live. Next, the willingness to choose to take this unknown scary path, with its thorns and potholes, possibly giving me a sprained ankle or tumbling me into the brambles along the way.

Along with choice came the faith that with the help of a Higher Power, I could change my destiny and be free!

Part 3
A New Beginning

58
What Now?

In 2015, having related the end of my 40-year journey of forgiveness to Rabbi David, he asked me a profound question, "What now?" Acknowledging the importance of his question, I told him, "I have to contemplate that."

Actually I had been wrestling with that question for quite a while. I was 87. *Why am I still here? I am the only one left of my family (the Goodmans, Twerskys, and Borkos) and most of my friends my age are gone.*"

I see the people around me going to and coming home from work, wheeling baby carriages, walking their dogs, coming from the playground with their toddlers, going shopping for food for the family and dinner parties, mail carriers delivering mail, delivery trucks coming and going, workmen building, renovating and repairing houses. They have a purpose in life. What is *my* purpose? I've done many of the things they aspire to or are doing. Why am I still here?

I've tasted many of life's pleasures: married my childhood sweetheart; become a mother and grandmother; traveled to all seven continents and 42 states; and had three fulfilling careers (teaching nursery school and kindergarten in Bed Stuy in Brooklyn, working as a TV producer for Channel 31, and also serving as Special Assistant to the Commissioner of the New York State Division of Human Rights).

I have given back to society and made visible, tangible changes to the New York City community: saving the Hunter College Campus Schools from extinction and making the high school co-ed; changing the requirements for men and consequently for women and Hispanics to become police officers; changing the rules so that people in wheelchairs could participate in the New York Marathon; being one of three women invited to become the first female members of the City Club of New York; and being elected a County Committeewoman for the Democratic Party on the Upper West Side, serving for the past 60 some odd years.

I had a summer home and the pleasures of country life: going barefoot, having a garden, swimming in the bay, beachcombing and walking by the ocean; waking up to the sound of the ocean; listening to the sounds of birds; picking beach plums, cranberries, strawberries and apples; eating freshly-caught fish and freshly-harvested fruits and vegetables; making beach plum and cranberry jam and apple upside-down cake; watching the fishing boats return; watching the gulls breaking clam shells on rooftops; having dinner at the beach and singing around a roaring fire while listening to the sound of the ocean; walking in the woods and watching sunsets at the bay.

I have been fortunate to have been loved and given love with passion.

I've had my share of grief as well: a particularly ugly breakup of a marriage and a long-time estranged adult son.

I'm blessed with good health, good friends and family, and have all my marbles. How can I serve?

I can serve by:

-continuing on my *sadhana* (spiritual journey)—there's always more schmutz to wash away

  -being aware of the goal of unity with the Divine

  -continuing to study Torah

  -sharing my wisdom and gaining wisdom from others

  -giving blessings and receiving blessings from others

  -seeing what kind of people my grandchildren become as adults:

their dreams, their careers, and their partners

-keeping the door open, without any expectations for a miraculous reconciliation with my son.

-enjoying each day as if it were my last, but with the intention of living to 100.

My prayer is for God to keep me healthy so I can do His/Her work.

When I asked the Guru in a letter how I could serve, she replied, " I remember you doing so-o-o much *seva* (selfless service). The best *seva* you can offer is to be happy and have a life filled with joy."

I no longer wrestle with the "why." I'm at peace knowing I have a new purpose in life.

59
A Perfect Day In An Imperfect Month

The day after Election Day, 2016, I looked at my calendar and was thrilled to see an entire morning and afternoon free of elections, doctor, therapy or pulmonary rehab appointments. Free to enjoy!

Christies, the art auction house, was holding an auction that night of high end paintings—among them a Monet priced at $81 million, a Matisse, a Picasso—and I wanted to see them. Although it might be too late for public viewing, I decided to take the chance.

I put on my elegant grey-wool cape, rather than my everyday jacket and wrapped myself in a colorful scarf so as to present myself as a picture of opulence and a possible buyer of expensive art. I made my way down to Rockefeller Plaza.

Getting off the subway at 50th Street, I realized I had left my folding chair home, without which I could not manage standing at an art gallery or museum. Since I couldn't go home to get it, I walked to the auction house upset, thinking that seeing something is better than missing out completely.

Sure enough my appearance worked. An employee came over to me as soon as I walked through the door and asked if I wanted to see the Impressionists. She also invited me to attend the afternoon auction being held at 2:00 PM. I followed her to a room where the Monet, "Grainstack," was illuminated and on display. Also welcoming me was a marvelous Marini sculpture, reminding me of the Marini I saw in Venice on the lawn of Peggy Guggenheim's home.

Getting off the vaporetto, one is greeted by a magnificent statue by Marino Marini. A horse and its rider—the rider with his head held high pointing upward—the horse flying through the air, his long tail and erect penis thrusting toward the sky. Only Peggy Guggenheim could greet her guests with such fun and such love of life.

The statue at Christies, alas, had no penis.

In this room there were other sculptures by Henry Moore, Degas and more painters. Other rooms had Tamayo, Botero, Picasso, Matisse, Cezanne, with enough benches for me to rest in between these magnificent servings of art.

On the mezzanine floor, I spotted the auction going on and went in. I had been to auctions in East Hampton, bidding and buying things like a tailor's dummy or old farm tools, but this was the real McCoy. It was a brand new experience for me to be among people bidding tens of thousands of dollars with a flick of the wrist, hardly thinking twice. And this was just the kiddy show. At night they would play at the auction with millions. I sat there enjoying the scene, savoring each moment and resting my tired body. It was great fun.

On the street leaving Christies, I noticed that the entire wall and ceiling of the exterior entrance was painted by Sol Lewitt, a wonderful colorist and one of my favorite modern painters.

I walked to the 50th street bus stop and a usually late #5 bus pulled up a few moments after I arrived. I used the half-hour on the bus to scribble, came home and took a nap.

The end of a perfect day!

No, just half of a perfect day; there was more to come.

I woke from my nap, had dinner and dressed for the Great Performers concert at Alice Tully Hall at Lincoln Center. I was to hear Jeremy Denk, a pianist I had never heard play before. I sat down in my usual great seat; left side, six rows from the front. I was in for a treat. He played for 80 minutes straight, without an intermission and without a score. He took the audience musically from the 1300s to 2016 with 23 composers. Imagine playing Beethoven, Mozart, Bach and then Stravinsky, Schoenberg and Philip Glass—without taking a breath.

The audience was mesmerized. Nobody moved, nobody coughed. He was magnificent, the best solo performance concert I had ever attended. He got four curtain calls—people couldn't stop applauding.

What a day! Something sorely needed a day after the trauma of Trump's election.

60
Mt. Sinai

Now that it is difficult for me to do extensive walking or standing, I take more cabs than in the past. The downside is that it is expensive; the upside is that I get to interact with a group of people I couldn't otherwise.

I like to talk with cab drivers, particularly because New York drivers are predominantly immigrants from all over the world. They are surprised and pleased when I tell them I have been to the country of their birth and interesting conversations follow.

One cab driver was from Egypt. Upon hearing that I had been to Egypt, he asked in a slightly challenging voice, "Have you been to Mt. Sinai?"

"Yes," I slowly answered with a smile. His question jogged my memory, reminding me of an experience I had not thought about for a long time.

When I was in Israel in the late 1970s, in my atheist days, it seemed likely that Mt. Sinai would be given to Egypt as part of the Peace Accords, and the Israelis I met urged me to visit before it was too late. I took their advice.

I signed up for a bus tour and was warned in advance that the trip was rugged with only the bare minimum necessities. I was not deterred. The bus drove through the Sinai desert for hours. Seeing nothing but sand and more sand for miles and miles, we would periodically come upon an overturned tank rusting in the hot sun, reminding us of the war with the Egyptians won by the Israelis.

We finally came to a mountain thought to be *the* Mt. Sinai. Almost at the top was Santa Katerina, a Russian Orthodox monastery, where we were to have dinner and spend the night before our journey very early the next morning. The mission of the monks of Santa Katerina was to keep watch over some of the most beautiful icons in the world which they kept hidden from view. Before we settled down to eat the kosher, bland, almost inedible boxed dinner brought from Tel Aviv, I cajoled one of the monks to show me some of the icons dating back to the seventh century. They were exquisite.

We slept on folding cots with only a small pillow and a thin blanket. Bare minimum it was. Not exactly the King David Hotel, but it was fine considering what lay ahead the next day.

In the morning I was given a choice—climb on foot to the summit or ride a donkey. Even though I was scared, I very reluctantly chose the donkey. I got on. It began to move under me, and I began to lose all sense of balance. I felt as if I was falling down one buttock at a time, panicked, and shouted for the donkey to stop. I got to my feet on terra firma as quickly as I could. It didn't matter how steep the climb; anything was better than riding the donkey.

Our goal was to reach the summit before sunrise. The walk was difficult, but we made it just in time. It was glorious! Standing on top of the mountain, looking out at the blue sky, the white clouds, and the sun coming up, I was on top of the world. Whether or not it really *was* Mt. Sinai I was standing on didn't matter. I *felt* it was Mt. Sinai.

At the very top was a small shrine with a white cross on it. Standing beside it was a young man with a yarmulke on his head wrapped in *tefillin* (phylacteries) and a *tallit* (prayer shawl) saying *shacharit* (morning prayers).

The sound of the prayer, the sound of silence, surrounded by the clouds, being higher than any visible mountain, I didn't have to be a believer to know I was in heaven.

61
Silent Retreats

Though I love retreats, they are getting harder for me physically. Bedtime is at 9:00 PM, lights out at 10, meditation at 6:00 AM, breakfast at 7. I'm a night owl, get a second wind at 10:00 PM and don't fall asleep until 2:00 AM. Many times I am up at 6 due to insomnia and do not fall asleep again til 7:30 AM. Nonetheless, on a retreat, I follow the schedule. Unfortunately, I am then prone to falling asleep during meditation sessions and am known to snore.

I particularly love silent retreats, and a few years ago, I was on a five-day silent retreat with The Institute of Jewish Spirituality in Garrison, New York, held in a former monastery overlooking the majestic Hudson River, facing West Point. The surroundings were beautiful.

At the last session of the retreat, the presenter said, "Talk to God. Out loud." It was a delicious idea. I had spoken to God before, inwardly, or in a whisper, but I had never really talked to Him/Her *out loud*. For some time now, I had been contemplating, "What is the purpose of my life? Why am I still here?" Wow, now I could ask God.

It was an autumn night, misty, foggy, with a very light drizzle. I walked into the fog and found myself in the center of the mist, a mist within a larger mist which separated itself and surrounded me. It reached up to the sky infinitely. I was in a tube or cylinder of mist just wide enough to embrace me. It was protecting me and loving me. I was cradled not only in the arms of a larger universe, but in a smaller universe all my own.

I began calling out in a loud voice, "God. Oh, God," but got no further. I began to sob. From deep inside, tears began to pour; tears of joy and gratitude. As I stood there in the Center of Love, I knew it was God. It was God telling me my life was worth living.

62

Pure Love

Although it was a glorious, sunny, clear, crisp autumn Shabbos morning, I walked along 105th Street on my way to shul with tears in my eyes. Along with Rosh Hashanah, my son Nick's 54th birthday was approaching, and I usually got teary every year at this time. He had been estranged from me for about 30 years, and although I sent him birthday greetings every year and tried to heal the rift, he rebuffed my attempts at reconciliation.

Today, other factors played a part in my sadness. I was reading "*Pumpkin Eaters*" by Matti Friedman about the war in Lebanon, of young Israeli boys ages 18, 19, and 20 dying needlessly and their mothers' heartbreak. Also, after three years of memoir writing, I finally started thinking and writing about Nick's estrangement and those thoughts and memories brought me to tears.

A perfect storm for sadness.

Sitting in shul, I thought: should I ignore my feelings and stay in gratitude for the good times I had parenting this little boy, or should I give into my sadness, cry, and come out on the other side?

My eyes closed and I fell into meditation. I saw my heart outside of my body, cleanly broken in half. Nick, as a boy, was put into one half of my heart and the other half was closed on top of it. Then an invisible hand began sewing up these two halves of my heart with Nick snugly inside. I was bathed in pure love.

After services, at kiddush, sitting at a table, I watched Ariel, the rabbi's wife, sitting at a table nearby with their three-month-old baby, Or, nursing and falling asleep in her arms. She was pure mother love. I watched her without tears, without nostalgia, without thinking about what I no longer had; just basking in the moment, enjoying her.

She was pure love, and so was I.

On that Rosh Hashanah I was given the honor of opening and closing the doors of the ark of the Torah. When it was time to bless the children, the space was filled with parents and children and me. I was happily surrounded and swallowed up in their midst and again spotted Ariel and baby Or. With a warm heart, I smiled.

I blessed them and also felt blessed in return.

63
Another Perfect Day

I was taking the Living Deeply workshop that met monthly at Romemu, given by Nili, an inspiring teacher, congregant and friend. At the beginning of the year, we participants randomly picked a *pasuk* (verse) from the Torah and studied it for the entire year. It was fascinating to watch it unfold and see how it was relevant in our everyday lives.

My verse was Exodus 21:7

When a man sells his daughter as a slave, she shall not be freed as male slaves are.

Along with an interpretation of relationships between fathers and daughters, I saw this as a tale of courage; a female finding ways to free herself from a male-controlled society. To me this was the epitome of courage, a quality I realized I had.

On my way to class on the Sunday of Memorial Day Weekend, I changed buses at 100th St and Broadway, not my usual route, and went into a Health Nuts store to buy some food for snack time. I bought two bananas and bumped into an acquaintance from my ashram world; seeing him was an unexpected treat. Outside the store, a man was begging, and when I shared my bananas with him, he blessed me.

I then walked down to Michael's (the Everything Store) at 100th and Columbus Ave, to buy artificial flowers to decorate a hat for a special occasion.

A week earlier my friend Cecile, one of the two remaining older friends I had left in New York, and I were talking about the olden days when we wore hats and white gloves and how it was fun to get dressed up. She called me the next day, all excited, "Let's get dressed in fancy hats like in the days of old and have tea."

"What a great idea," I said, "How about lunch at the Boathouse in Central Park?"

We chose a date and called for reservations.

I found the perfect pink flowers to put on my hat and walked to Central Park West where I could catch a bus to 110th St. I was getting tired, very tired. Walking and standing had become a chore rather than the pleasure it once was, and I was looking forward to the bus ride. I arrived at the Central Park West corner only to find it cordoned off. The policeman said it was the last block of a parade and the street was closed! The Central Park West bus was not running! As I stood there wondering how I would get to 110th St, the policeman told me to walk. I laughed at the idea of walking 10 blocks. What was I to do?

From out of nowhere a cab came by. My savior!

As I sat in my chariot, I began talking to the driver, who had a thick accent.

"What is your native language?"

"Urdu."

"Where are you from?"

"Pakistan."

"What is your name?"

"Sadiq!"

I gulped. The driver said *Sadiq* in Urdu means "true-hearted;" (the same word *tzadik* in Hebrew means "Righteous One"). *Tzadik* was used to refer to the Berditchever Rebbe who was known for his compassion and was called "the Righteous One."

Rescued by a Sadiq! Protected by my *zayde*!

At the workshop I read a chapter about courage from my memoir. It was about when my marriage was breaking up at the same time the contractor of the house we were building in Amagansett ran off with our money. Instead of wallowing in anguish, I refinanced the mortgage, got the house built, and with the remaining money took the children to Europe on an adventure.

The class not only marveled at my courage and enjoyed hearing of my European experiences, but praised my writing.

One of the people in the group, a good friend of mine, shared the dire financial circumstances she and her husband were experiencing, including the threat of eviction. After the workshop was over, I quietly offered to lend them money to pay the coming month's rent on their apartment.

I received and I gave. It felt good.

64
Unexpected Blessings

I was in a pulmonary rehab gym, an unlikely place to meet people from my ashram world.

A woman came up to me with an exuberant "hello."

I smiled and said, "hello" back, but had no idea who she was.

"Do you recognize me?"

I looked at her blankly.

"The ashram," she said.

I still didn't recognize her. She went on, "I did what you suggested, and it changed my life."

I answered sheepishly, "Remind me." I still didn't have a clue.

She began the story. "We were standing on a line waiting for food at the ashram. I told you about a house I saw in Staten Island. I couldn't afford it but I wanted to buy it. You quickly, quietly and firmly said "buy it." At the time I couldn't see how, but I took your advice. Now, four years later, it's worth almost twice what I paid for it. It has a basement which I turned into a meditation room and later was converted into a meditation center. Thank you. Thank you."

Then she said, "You're a writer." I was puzzled and wondered how she knew I was writing.

"I didn't write back then," I said.

"Yes, you did. You wrote letters to the Guru."

She reminded me that I *did* write letters to the Guru, but in my eyes, that didn't make me a writer.

"You're right" I answered. "How did you know?"

"One was read out loud. It was after the Month Long Course."

I then remembered that after receiving my permission, a swami had read my letter to the Guru thanking her for the course. It was at a program with a thousand people in attendance and was a big honor. I was thrilled and taken by surprise.

The woman continued, "When a letter is read aloud you never know who will hear it. I heard it and remembered."

"Thanks for your kind words," I said humbly. "As a matter of fact, I have been writing my memoir."

"That's great. You're a good writer. You have a lot to say and have a wonderful sense of humor. Keep writing."

"Thanks. Thanks so much."

I was touched by her words that had come out of the blue. I felt the Guru was showering me with blessings, supporting me, and encouraging me in my writing.

65
Scary Can Be Fun

I read in a travel magazine that the scariest place on earth is standing on the top of Chichen Itza, one of the tallest pyramids in Mexico, looking down. Yes, it is scary. I was there. I climbed that pyramid at age 72. Climbing up was scary enough. With my traveling companion at the base of the pyramid watching me, I began the climb. Behind me was a group of twenty-somethings, who, when they heard how old I was, were impressed. About two-thirds of the way up, climbing on all-fours, I got very tired and shouted to them, "I don't think I'm going to make it."

They urged me on, "Yes you can, you're almost there."

We made it to the top and looked down. Yes, the scene below *was* scary. Looking down, terra firma seemed miles away, the people were tiny, the steps were never-ending and there were no ropes.

I said the mantra, asked for Divine help and climbed down backwards, looking straight ahead and not daring to look down. It was the first pyramid I climbed, but not my last.

But the scariest place ever? NO!

The scariest place ever was doing a very mundane action—crossing the street. However, no ordinary street. It was crossing the street in Hanoi, the capital of Vietnam. The motorbikes and bicycles whizzed by, never stopping to allow pedestrians to cross. There were no traffic lights, and if by chance there was one, nobody obeyed it. Bikes rounded the corner into traffic without stopping. Seeing this speeding wave of bikes coming straight at us, Yetta and I stood at the curb, frozen. Yes, it was scary and we were afraid to move even though we were told we would be safe if we just walked.

"Walk straight ahead but under *no* circumstances stop. Walk into the traffic, look straight ahead and keep going."

Easy for them to say. We were petrified.

We looked at each other, locked arms, laughed a little hysterical laugh and with a sigh of, "Oh well," and a shoulder shrug said, "Let's go."

Looking neither left nor right, slowly putting one foot in front of the other, we started walking into traffic as the bicycles zoomed by. Once again I said the mantra, this time louder than at Chichen Itza, and off we went, slowly, carefully, sure this was our last moment on earth.

Incredibly, what we were told was true. Somehow, the bikes swerved around us without banging into each other, and we made it to the other side of the street. We looked at each other, smiled, breathed a sigh of relief, and burst into laughter.

66
The SAJ Spring Retreat

There is a joke about the Jewish man who was marooned on a desert island for many years. He was finally rescued and was proudly showing his rescuers around the island, pointing to all that he had built in order to stay alive. He said, "This is my hut. This is the building where I kept the animals I caught." Pointing to two other buildings, he said, "This is the shul I pray in. And the other is the shul I don't go to."

I am just the opposite. I belong to two synagogues, Romemu and the SAJ. Although I am no longer an active member of the SAJ, I have roots going back 18 years that I still want to nurture. I, being a retreat junkie, whenever the SAJ goes on retreat, I am there.

At the 2016 spring retreat held in Pennsylvania, we broke into workshops, one of which was improv. Improv fascinates me; it also scares me to death. Having been married to an actor-writer-director and being surrounded by professional actors until age 40, I didn't dare go to an improv class and expose myself to being seen as an amateur. Although I am also frozen with the fear of letting myself go, I've always had a secret wish to try improv in a room with non-professionals. Lynn and Sam Cohen, professional actors and teachers, were leading the session on improv. This retreat was the perfect time.

Instead of seizing this opportunity, I chose something safe, a book discussion with Diane and Nancy, the people who lead the book group I have belonged to for many years. Sitting in the room, waiting for the session to begin, I kept thinking about the improv group meeting across the road. I *really* wanted to try it, but it was an enormous challenge to my sense of wellbeing. Sitting in this room, I felt fear had won. I felt I was letting myself down; I was being a coward.

And then I did it! I gritted my teeth, picked myself up, and took my very frightened self across the road. Believe me when I say it took guts; I was both scared and excited at the same time.

The session was nothing like I imagined. No one-on-one scenes to improvise. No wannabe actors to compete with. Just improvisational exercises for fun. I enjoyed myself immensely, so much so I invited them to give this workshop to the "Aging to Sageing" group at Romemu. It felt good facing my fears and trying something new and challenging at age 88. To top it off, I had fun!

At the last short service of the retreat led by Rabbi Lauren, she said, "Anyone who has done something for the first time during this retreat, come up for an *aliyah.*" (a blessing at the altar.)

Not only did I have the inner satisfaction of doing something brave, I even received a blessing from God!

67
Double Blessings

My accidentally flooding the bathroom was a blessing in disguise. The water, lots of it, flowed into my bedroom, which led to new partial sub-flooring and flooring, new carpeting, bookcases to be emptied and moved and a paint job. A monumental, unexpected, but necessary task nonetheless, paid for by my home insurance.

My bedroom is the place for sleeping, writing, meditating, (alas, no longer for lovemaking.) Overflowing with books and papers, it needed a facelift for a very long time.

The workmen were working in the apartment for a week, and we became friendly. One, Billy, told me about his year-and-a-half-old baby, the baby's mother (not his wife), and his buying a new house. When he came back from a break, smelling of cigarettes, me, an ex-smoker, who kicked the habit at age 41 during the breakup of her marriage, on the third try, said to him:

"You smoke."

"How can you tell?"

"I smell it."

He said sheepishly: "I tried to stop last year, but it lasted a week. I can't stop."

"I know," I replied. "I found trying didn't help me, either. I stopped when I looked at myself seriously and only when I made a promise to myself to stop, was I able to kick it."

"I can't."

"Can you promise your lady friend?"

"I can't. It's too hard."

"Do you think your baby deserves to have a father while he's growing up?"

He looked at me and thought for a while.

"Do you think you can promise *him*? Can you do it for your son's sake?"

He thought a little longer and then painfully said: "I just can't."

"Maybe at some time later on," I said and dropped the subject.

Six weeks later, I got a phone call. "Ms Goodman, it's Billy. I want to tell you I stopped smoking. I went over to my little boy, took his hand, and looked deeply into his eyes: "'I promise you I will never smoke again.' And I stopped.

"A few days later I had a big fight with his mother. I thought: 'One cigarette won't hurt.' I went to buy a pack but when I got to the store I turned around and went home. I survived without a cigarette and haven't touched one since."

68
We Can Bless Each Other

Simchas Torah (celebration of the Torah) is a holiday of rejoicing, dancing and embracing the Torah during a long night's celebration.

It was *Simchas Torah* at Romemu. The Torah was taken out of the ark, and Rabbi David called upon the oldest congregants to hold the Torah and begin the dancing. I, along with the other octogenarians, went up to the *Bima*, and the Torah was put into my arms. It was very, very heavy. Arlene, an old friend from my ashram world who was unexpectedly next to me, held a part of the Torah which made it light enough for me to carry. For the first time I was able to dance with the Torah around the entire synagogue. What a joy!

When I put the Torah down—because I couldn't dance standing on my feet any longer—I sat down and danced in my chair.

David said, "Empty yourselves and allow the Torah in."

I closed my eyes and became empty. The Torah was there—inside me.

Then I saw I was in Berditchev in Rabbi Levi Yitzhak's synagogue. He was dancing with the Torah, and his Hasidim were dancing around him in a circle. I was there. I was Torah. I had no body. It was ecstasy.

I opened my eyes and I was in Romemu. I closed them and I was with the Rebbe. I didn't want it to end. But it did end and another beautiful experience began. David unfurled the Torah, and each person held on to a portion. The entire congregation was wrapped inside it as they held it. The synagogue was bathed in pure love.

We were invited to choose a *pasuk* (Torah portion) to study and live with for the year.

My *pasuk* was from Genesis 48:14.

"And Israel stretched out his right hand and laid it upon Ephraim's head, who was the younger, and his left hand upon Manassah's head guiding his hands unwittingly; for Manassah was the first born."

I asked Amichai, one of the scholars who was there to explain the pasukim to the congregants, what he thought it meant, and he said I would get unexpected blessings and to love my children equally.

I told him of my experience with the Torah and the Rebbe. He then surprised me by asking me to bless him. I put my hand on his head, and he did the same to me. It brought me to tears reminding me of Nicky's Bar Mitzvah. At the time, I was an atheist, but when the rabbi put his hand on Nicky's head to bless him, tears came to my eyes. Whenever I go to a Bar or Bat Mitzvah and the rabbi blesses the child this way, it moves me to tears.

Our hands were on each other's heads; we stayed in time that did not exist. When we came out of it, I told Amichai I saw us dancing and praying together in Rabbi Levi Yitzhak's house. He smiled, we hugged and parted.

69
Shabbat Comes Early

On a beautiful sunny Friday afternoon, I was sitting in an outdoor cafe overlooking Delray Beach, Florida, with my friend Valerie, before taking a walk on the beach. I smelled tobacco smoke. There was an attractive middle-aged couple sitting at a table near us, and I saw that the man was sneaking a cigarette — taking a puff and hiding the culprit under the table.

I presumed smoking was allowed outdoors and that I had to put up with the smoke. When the waiter came up to him and pointedly said he had to put out the cigarette, the man sheepishly left the table. His companion turned to us and told us his story. He was her husband and he had stopped smoking 20 years earlier but started again after his father had died. She was visibly upset.

He came back, joined our conversation and said proudly, "My father died two years ago, and I began smoking again."

"Do you want to join him?" I asked, smiling.

He laughed and said "yes" and began wise-cracking about his imminent death. And then, out of the blue, he turned to me and asked, "Are you going to shul tonight?" It was erev (eve of) Shabbat.

Surprised, I said, "yes."

He told me he was orthodox, and he didn't smoke on Shabbos.

I said, "Do you believe every day is Shabbos?" (as some Hasidim would say).

"Yes."

"Well, then," I said mischievously with a big grin, "If every day is Shabbos, then you can't smoke."

He smiled, nodded his head like he understood. He heard me, but he wouldn't listen as he continued joking.

They left a short while later. We said goodbye and laughingly, I said, "Remember, every day is Shabbos."

As they walked away still laughing, his wife turned and gave me a thumbs up.

70
Down Under

One beautiful autumn day I got to thinking about New Zealand and its breathtaking beauty—its pristine blue lakes and majestic mountain peaks. Autumn is spectacular everywhere in the world, but the comparatively less spoiled places, like New Zealand, Alaska and Antarctica, stand out in my mind.

The next evening I found myself at an off-Broadway theater to see a play about Albania during World War II and the lesser-known story of how that tiny country saved its Jews. Waiting for the curtain to go up, I was approached by a woman with a huge smile, "Hello. You're Evelyn."

"Yes." I was surprised. How did she know my name?

"Do you remember me?"

I stared blankly. "I'm afraid not."

"We were together on a trip to New Zealand three years ago. I'm Helen Brown."

I smiled, "Now I remember you." I did, but only vaguely. "Funny, I was thinking of New Zealand just yesterday."

We began talking and I changed my seat to sit with Helen and her husband. We shared warm, happy memories of the trip but our conversation was cut short when the play began. After the curtain came down, I thought we could continue reminiscing but they lived in Westchester and had to hurry to catch a train. We said good night and I took a cab home.

In the taxi, still thinking of New Zealand, it brought to mind an incident I didn't want to remember. When I travel I tend to forget unpleasant experiences. I forget that many times I have back pain or upper respiratory infections or that I come back with bronchitis or even pneumonia. This particular incident was not the part of the trip I chose to remember.

My traveling companions and I were on a spiritual trip to spend time with Auntie, a woman who was a shaman in the tradition of the indigenous Maori people and held in highest esteem. We were at her home in a large indoor/outdoor room sitting on the floor in a semi circle around her chair. She talked for a while about things I have subsequently forgotten, but then said something I shall never forget.

"The Israelis knew about the 9/11 bombing of the World Trade Center and there were no Jews killed that morning because of advanced notice."

Shock and anger overwhelmed me as I heard this anti-Semitic filth from someone who was supposed to be an evolved person. How could this be?

I knew I had to speak out, but how do you challenge a person so well-respected and with so much authority? I sat there in pain, fuming with anger; it shocked and hurt me. And it was very scary. How could I keep my anger from interfering with an effective response?

By the time she finished talking, I had recovered my composure and raised my hand.

"I am sitting here, very upset, very sad at what I heard you say about the Jews, and that this ugly, vicious anti-Semitic lie has traveled halfway around the world. It's hard to believe that this poison is being repeated here and it shocks me." Sadly, on that day, I lost a friend/fellow congregant in my synagogue, and a neighbor in my apartment building, both Jews.

The room got very quiet.

Unfortunately, I don't remember what she said in response. When the group dispersed, the Jews in the group came up to me and one said, "That took guts. I was afraid to say anything. Thanks for doing it for me."

A second one said, "Thanks for speaking up, I wanted to but didn't know how."

A third said, "I didn't see anything wrong with what she said." That response from a Jew saddened me even more.

I learned many years ago from the ADL (Anti-Defamation League) never to let an anti-Semitic or racist remark go by without challenging it. But I didn't expect to have to do so in New Zealand on a spiritual journey to a spiritual leader.

Ironically, this ugly incident came to mind after seeing a poignant, beautiful play about brave, good-hearted, kind people who saved Jews during World War II at their peril. In the play, a true story was depicted about a family who was hiding a Jewish teenage boy. They, too, had a teenage boy. A neighbor turned them in and told the Nazis they had only one son. The Nazis broke into their home and demanded the Jewish boy. It is impossible to believe that they gave up their own son instead. But they did!

From New Zealand, I flew to Australia, this time to visit friends, Steve and Amanda. Sitting in the cab from the airport to Sydney, I started talking to the cab driver as is my wont.

"How's the weather?"

"Good."

"I'm visiting Australia for 10 days. I'm from New York, and I'm excited to be in Sydney."

He warmly welcomed me to his city. Although the conversation that ensued was mundane, I enjoyed listening to his accent. By the time we arrived at the hotel it was late at night, and I was travel-weary, jet-lagged and hungry. To my chagrin, the kitchen was closed, and my room was on the third floor in a building with no elevator. The lone man at the desk suggested a food market that was open.

I dragged myself into a cab and asked the driver to take me to the market. We arrived, but not before we chatted about Sydney and how excited I was to be there. "The first thing tomorrow morning I'm going to the aquarium. I'm looking forward to seeing the sea life you have in the Sydney waters." He looked at me as if to say, 'These crazy Americans,' but instead said, "Don't miss the harbor," in the accent I so enjoyed as he dropped me off. "You're lucky, it's the only market open in these parts."

In the market I chose some fruit, cheese and biscuits. At the counter, wanting to pay, I realized I had no purse. I had left it in the cab! In my purse was my passport, traveler's checks, Australian and U.S. money, and plane tickets. *Everything* was in the purse.

The owners of the market tried their best to console me. They sat me down and urged me to eat while they called the police who tried to track down the taxi I rode in. No such luck. After a futile search, they apologized and drove me back to the hotel.

On the ride back I thought of tomorrow and how I would spend one of my very precious days in Sydney at the American Embassy, bank and airline office trying to get a new passport, money and plane ticket home. Outwardly I was calm as I usually am in an emergency, but I was really upset. What an inauspicious way to start my visit to Australia.

Back at the hotel, I slowly walked the three flights up to my room, undressed and got into bed, still very worried. I finally fell into a fitful sleep when I heard a knock at the door. Groggily, I stumbled out of bed. Who could it be? I opened the door and to my delight, there stood the cab driver holding my purse!

"I found the bag in the back of my cab. I remembered our conversation about the aquarium and wondered where I picked up that nice American tourist lady," he said as he handed me my purse.

"Thanks, thanks!" I excitedly said. "I'd like to give you something for your trouble."

I wanted to give him some money but was careful not to insult him. As I opened my purse he said, "No ma'am, I was happy to do it."

I insisted, "Please, take something."

He insisted, "No."

I thanked him again, we shook hands and he left.

I was euphoric and wondered—if this had happened to a tourist in New York City, would the cab driver have done the same?

I think so.

I hope so.

I *know* so. Recently, I left my camera in a cab coming home from the Jewish Heritage Museum in lower Manhattan. I was the driver's last fare before going home to Brooklyn after a hard day's work. He called to tell me he had found my camera. The next morning, before he started work, he went out of his way, and drove to my apartment in Manhattan to return my camera. He, too, refused any money.

71
Queen for a Night

In 1993, when I was young and 65, I met Yetta on an Elderhostel trip to Bali. Even though she lived in Arizona and me in New York, we became friends and traveling companions. Now that we were both turning 90, we decided to celebrate and take another Elderhostel (now called Road Scholar) trip going on a paddle boat up the Mississippi, starting in New Orleans and ending in Memphis.

I looked forward to being in New Orleans again and eating in one of the city's marvelous renowned restaurants. Commander's Palace and Arnaud's (which had a jazz band as well as good food) were among those highly recommended. Although I was making reservations months in advance, I was told the jazz band's room was completely booked. Since I couldn't make a choice between the two at that time, I made a reservation for both restaurants, postponing my decision until I arrived in New Orleans.

Arnaud's, on Bienville near Bourbon Street, was three blocks from the hotel, and I thought it would be a good idea to walk over and speak to the powers that be in person. When I told the woman at the desk that my friend and I were celebrating our 90th birthdays, I got the usual, "No way! Wow!" And then she said, "I'll have a table for you in the Jazz Room."

I was delighted and thanked her profusely.

"Would you like balloons?"

With an enthusiastic shake of my head, I said, "Absolutely."

I had obviously decided on Arnaud's as the place for our celebration and walked back to the hotel with a big smile. I would give the coveted Commander's Palace reservation to some lucky person on our tour.

The next night, dressed for the occasion, Yetta and I entered the restaurant. Seated near the door at a round table were eight young, attractive women wearing long-haired green, blue, purple, pink and orange wigs. We burst out laughing and stopped at the table to admire the wigs and talk. They were a bachelorette party and were partying big time. When they heard we were celebrating our 90th birthdays, they didn't believe it. We looked so young. Two women tried their wigs on us, and we joined in the fun. We all took pictures together and chatted. They had come from all over the country to celebrate their friend's wedding. One woman turned out to be a neighbor, living on 70th Street and Columbus Avenue on the Upper West Side.

The bride turned to me, "What are you drinking?"

I answered, "I'm not drinking."

She repeated, "What are you drinking?"

"I don't drink anymore."

"Come on, it's a party, what are you drinking?"

I finally gave in, "A coconut mojito." I had tasted it a few nights before at my grandson Ross's graduation party and it was delicious.

"Come to my wedding!"

"Where is it?"

"Palo Alto."

And I meant it when I answered, "I would if it were geographically possible."

They were thrilled about our ages and fussed over us a while longer.

We were then seated at a table close to the band near a window. The promised red balloons were tied to our chairs. We sat down and as we began to order dinner, two complimentary mojitos came to our table from the women. We turned to thank them, holding up our glasses; they raised theirs in return. When the women finished their dinner they came over to our table to hug and kiss us again and repeated that we were their inspiration. *They* were an inspiration to *me*—independent, professional, successful young women.

The band—a piano, banjo and bass—was really good. They played not only jazz, but also "Happy Birthday" and asked us to come on to the bandstand where more pictures were taken. Other guests in the restaurant, hearing the singing and looking at us, came over to wish us happy birthday. Some even hugged us. All were amazed at our age.

When it came time to pay the check, the waiter said, "Put your charge cards away; the bill has been taken care of by the women." Our mouths dropped open wide. What a wonderful, beautiful, generous surprise!

As we walked out of the restaurant we passed the desk staff again, they again wished us happy birthday and the female manager said she hoped we were pleased. We sure were!

I walked out still in shock, savoring the love that was heaped upon us.

Our next stop was Fritzel's Pub, a renowned jazz joint on Bourbon Street. On this Saturday night, Bourbon Street was as crowded as Times Square on New Year's Eve, with revelers celebrating the 300th anniversary of New Orleans. We were approached by people wanting to know the significance of the red balloons. When we told them it was our 90th birthday, they showered us with Mardi Gras beads and more hugs and kisses.

"Can I hug you?"

"Can I kiss you?"

"Of course!" I can never get enough hugs.

Yetta said, "Evelyn, look up!"

I looked up at the balconies. People were throwing us kisses and as they threw us more beads, I felt like a celebrity. Never before had I got as many hugs and kisses and unconditional love from strangers. It was exquisite to feel the love and genuine heartfelt goodwill from people I didn't know who felt like family, all ages, all colors and all sexual orientations. This truly was America!

It took 30 minutes for us to walk the four blocks to Fritzel's. The maître d' told us they were full and seated us at the door to wait until the band finished their set. When I exuberantly said, "It's our 90th birthday celebration," she smiled, left and told us to wait. Five minutes later she returned and seated us near the band, who proceeded to play "Happy Birthday."

The band leader announced our names, turned to me and asked, "Evelyn, what are you doing after the show?" He then asked for requests. Someone asked for "*When the Saints Come Marching In.*" The band leader said, "It's the second most popular request; the first is "*Happy Birthday.*"

It was great fun, great jazz, and we stayed for two more sets.

When it was time to go home, I said to Yetta, "Let's not go back on Bourbon Street. I don't want to spoil our experience. It's too perfect just the way it is."

I floated along the four blocks back to the hotel on quiet Royal Street. The perfect end to a remarkable evening.

Queen for a night! What a way to start the celebration of my 90th birthday!

72
Mystery of Miracles

There is nothing worse that can happen to a parent than the death of a child. The next worst thing is for a child to be estranged. The heart is truly broken. It never heals; there is no scar. The best that can happen is the formation of a hard scab, which enables a person to live everyday life without an open wound. That scab can be pulled away when confronted with life—memories, rebuffs or rejections—and the pain comes rushing to the surface. The pain never really goes away.

Unfortunately I have a son living in Los Angeles who has been estranged for about 30 years. I can enjoy watching mothers with babies or little children in loving situations. I can feel happy for friends when I see close relationships with their grown children. But when I personalize it, go inside and experience what I am missing, my eyes well up with tears.

I think of the time Nicky was six months old, and Phil and I were separated for the first time. Nicky was teething and crying and I walked him in the middle of the night, holding him in my arms, singing to him to console him (against advice from friends to let him cry it out.) I wanted to cry with him, feeling the pain of being abandoned with two little children, and for him, an innocent, unaware of being abandoned by his father.

I remember the little boy I loved and wanted so desperately, putting his head on my lap one day in the middle of a conversation, looking up at me lovingly saying, "We will always live together." And me, foolish me, wanting him to be able to separate when the time came without guilt said, "We can live near each other, but when you grow up you will have a home of your own."

My mistake. For fear of being overprotective and smothering like my father was to me, I didn't tell him of the beauty, comfort, and fidelity of family love, but only about separation. I was at fault minimizing the loyalty and protection of unconditional familial love.

It has come back to haunt me.

I think of that loving little boy who wanted to live with me forever turning into someone who by age 17 never wanted to see me again. What happened? I continue to wonder. How could this happen?

He sure as hell was dealt a rotten deck of cards at birth. Notwithstanding that his father was highly intelligent and multi-talented—actor, writer, director, musician, artist—he was also someone who at Nicky's birth said to me, "I can't be a father to a boy." By the time Nicky was six months old, Phil ran off to England with a South African woman, and we were separated for six months. By the time Nicky was five, the marriage was still rocky, and the split was permanent by age seven. This time his father was discovered with the 15-year-old babysitter.

I was devastated. My childhood sweetheart, whom I loved more than life itself, was not only unfaithful, but with a child—wayward—but nonetheless, a child. I was angry, bitter, hurt, demeaned and ashamed. The betrayal was profound.

I wasn't the best of mothers. Heartbroken, I did a lot of crying, yelling and screaming at two innocent children while trying to keep things together.

Yes, I wasn't the emotional rock I should have been. Yes, I yelled. Yes, I was demanding and controlling—to keep everything from falling apart. But yes, I was also loving and caring, bringing fun into their lives and someone the children could depend upon.

All quite normal.

By age 13, headstrong and rebellious as teenagers can be, Nicky didn't do his homework and didn't abide by other family rules. His hormones raged, as they do in 13-year-olds, and by 14, was experimenting with sex as teens will do in ways that pushed the envelope. All normal teen behavior.

But somehow things snowballed, and we didn't come out okay on the other side. He turned into someone with a great deal of anger who wanted nothing to do with me. Why and how this estrangement has lasted this long is a mystery I wish I understood. However, instead of dwelling in the past, I keep trying to heal the rift.

It was hard to knowingly put myself in a position of being rejected, but I did it over and over again in the hopes that one day things would change and there would be a rapprochement. I had written him letters many times, apologizing for any hurt I had unwittingly caused him, had tried by phone and email to contact him, and even gone to Los Angeles for possible get-togethers, but to no avail. When I called, if he picked up, he would tell me after a few minutes that he had to go back to work and would hang up. He usually would not pick up the phone at all, and I would get his answering machine. I still sent him birthday wishes every year, along with my love, which although ignored, would always be there.

It seemed hopeless and I had just about given up making contact. However, remembering the efficacy of the mantra, I decided on one last try. Since Rosh Hashanah (the Jewish New Year), whenever I pictured Nick in my head, I added the mantra.

On January 1st, 2016, I went to the ashram. Waiting for the annual New Year's program to begin, I pictured Nick and using the mantra, I said to myself, "Breathe in the love; breathe out the poison." Nick's mouth turned into a big furnace, and I was shoveling the mantra into his mouth. I was breathing him.

In the program, the Guru offered this teaching,

"Breathe in deeply the fragrance of the heart."

I was astounded, realizing I was breathing in the message even before it had been spoken! Tears filled my eyes. To me it was an affirmation that maybe something would change!

Two weeks later at the synagogue it was the time in the service for the blessing of the children. I was watching the sweet scene of parents with children ranging from three months to 14 years, being blessed by Rabbi David. I remember Rabbi Shelly Zimmerman putting his hand on Nicky's head and blessing him at his Bar Mitzvah. This quiet act of love always moves me to tears.

Along with the parents blessing their children, I began blessing Nick in absentia while repeating the mantra. I then had a vision of the Guru sitting on her chair watching us. The Berditchever Rebbe came and put his hands on Nick's head and blessed him. I started to weep. Without touching me, he blessed me too. How beautiful, how touching, how unexpected. I sat amidst pure love, shedding tears of love and gratitude. I was being showered with blessings, the fruits of the mantra.

I had new hopes; maybe something would change. I decided to try again to reach out to Nick and planned a trip to L.A. in July. If nothing else, *I had changed*. I was going with no expectations. Although I would make every effort to see Nick, whatever happened would be okay. Also, the mantra was now my constant companion, and I packed it in my suitcase along with my purple Birkenstock sandals. I would travel with the mantra without expectations.

Beginning in March, in preparation for my visit, I began sending love to Nick in the form of the mantra. It was like the story of Yudhishthira, who hurled the powerful weapon, the astra, and was the hero of the Mahabharata, the epic story of India. At bedtime, I would repeat the mantra and wrap him in it, saying, breathe in the love, breathe out the pain. Breathe in the love, breathe out the hate. I would do the same in the morning when I awoke and later in the day whenever I thought of it. I would send the mantra with no expectation; just sending it with a mother's love for her son.

I was going to L.A. to visit my friend Cori, who, when she was four, was in my kindergarten class and was now almost 70 and a grandma. Two days before I left, I sent Nick an email telling him when I would be available for a possible visit. I left with no reply.

A few days later, I got an email, "Where in L.A. will you be?"

In response, I called him, not on my phone, but on Cori's phone so he wouldn't know it was me and pick up. I got a very cold "Hello" and I shriveled. He said it might be possible to see me the following week if he didn't need to work overtime, and then, in the middle of a sentence, he hung up. The hurt was enormous. I said, "This is it, I've had it. No more."

Cori encouraged me to call him back and pretend we got disconnected. I took her advice. I got his answering machine. I repeated that I would be available July 12, 13, and 14, but felt this was it. This was my last overture.

The next day I got an email, "Pencil in Thursday, July 13, for dinner if I'm not working." I was happy, continued to surround Nick with the mantra, but did not hold my breath.

On Thursday morning, July 13 at 8 o'clock, I got an email saying, "I made a reservation for three for dinner at 8:00 PM tonight at Anarbagh, an Indian restaurant in Beverly Hills." I was delighted. Dinner for three meant his wife Hortencia was coming. That was good; I liked her, and she would act as a buffer. He had chosen an Indian restaurant, I felt, to please me. It did.

I went to the restaurant with complete equanimity. I wasn't nervous, happy, or filled with expectation. I was there just to enjoy a dinner—no more. We had a marvelous dinner! We didn't talk about the past or the future. Rather, we were just telling stories, sitting around talking like friends do.

At one point Nick asked me, "Have you seen *Hamilton*?"

"Yes."

"With the original cast?"

"Yes. Something happened between me and Lin-Manuel Miranda. Would you like to hear it?"

"Sure."

I told Nick about Lin-Manuel Miranda saying on "Charlie Rose" that getting into Hunter High School had changed his life.

"I didn't know he went to Hunter," Nick replied, remembering how he was in the first class of boys at Hunter.

"Yes. I wrote Lin-Manuel a letter telling him of my part in getting the boys into the high school and feeling a tiny bit responsible for the creation of *"Hamilton."* Lin-Manuel answered with a very gracious letter thanking me for all my boys. The TV was on while I was opening his letter and there was Lin-Manuel on TV! Since I don't believe in coincidences, I wrote him again and told him so."

With that, Nick said, "Neither do I."

That started us on a conversation about synchronistic experiences.

Hortencia related a very improbable story about her being given a much sought-after ticket to a big concert at the Hollywood Bowl by a DJ she had called on a whim. Through a series of L. A. traffic miracles, she had managed to drive across town to meet the DJ's deadline and secure the tickets exactly on time. When the usher, impressed by her fabulous seat in the front row, said to her, "You must know someone very high up." She smiled and answered, "Yes. The Highest."

We were talking like like-minded people on the same vibration.

They wanted to hear about my trips. It was then I asked Nick if he had read the account of our trip to Europe I had sent him.

"Yes."

"What did you think?"

"It's more of a travelogue than a memoir."

"Why? You're in it."

"There wasn't much about me."

I realized then he had just skimmed it. I said, "Yes, you are." But instead of letting that turn into a confrontation which it easily could have, I turned to Hortencia and said, "This little boy, age 7, stood at the pool, chased me and Jody away, and taught himself to dive."

She was impressed. Nick said, "Well, you have to learn *sometime*," making light of his achievement.

I then told Hortencia how, when I was telling the children about the Spanish Inquisition I had asked, "What do you think happens to a country that treats people badly because of their religion?" This same little boy answered, "That country goes down."

At one point Nick looked at me and said, "You aged well, not like Phil. You don't mind me talking about him, do you?"

"No, not at all," I answered honestly.

Nick began a tirade against Phil, "For the last ten years of his life, he was dreadful—demanding, loud, yelling, nasty. He came into the world with no control, and that's how he left." Nick was visibly upset.

Using this as an opportunity to show him I forgave Phil, I said, "I'm sorry to hear this. Jody sat shiva for him in Washington. I went and shared with people about his marvelous sense of humor. I was sad that people didn't know that about him."

Hortencia added, turning to Nick, "He gave you good genes. You're smart and talented."

I said to Hortencia, "When Nick was two, he would pull up his stool and help me cook. I was a very good cook. Jody is now a marvelous cook. Phil was a fabulous cook, but Nick topped even him."

Nick interjected, "No, not really."

"Yes, really."

Hortencia snuggled up to him and said, "He's great. I don't want to share him with anyone."

I smiled, "It makes me very happy to see you happy."

They both thanked me.

Hortencia shared she was fifth generation Southwest American on her father's side and first generation on her mother's, and she spent many summers in the Baja in Mexico. At this point, after asking if they were interested, I related my experience with the whales in the Baja.

The evening went like that. We just told stories for two short hours until Nick abruptly said they had to leave and ended the evening. Hortencia apologized by saying they had to get up early the next morning.

I thanked them for the visit and said, "I hope we can do this again."

Hortencia said, "In L.A.?"

I said, "In L.A., New York, or on the phone."

They didn't reply.

Hortencia kissed me on both cheeks; Nick hugged me and put me into a Via cab which he ordered and paid for.

I floated into the cab in awe and gratitude. Even though I didn't expect anything further to happen, I didn't rule out the possibility.

I was not ecstatic, just content that there had been a rapprochement.

I was basking in the wonderment of it all, in a place of pure joy, a place of miracles!

Three miracles in my life:

Forgiving the Nazis.

Forgiving my ex-husband.

And now, having dinner with my son.

Thank you God, You Majestic, Divine Maker of Miracles!

I was jolted out of my reverie by the voice of the cab driver, starting a conversation. Somehow we got on the subject of meditation. He said he always wanted to try it but felt it was too complicated to do properly. I told him it really was simple. All he had to do was to sit up straight, focus on his breath, and if thoughts came up, to let them go like clouds in the sky.

He was eager to try it. At my destination, before getting out of the cab, at his request I guided him in a five-minute meditation, after which he said, "I felt like a tree and my worries, like the leaves, just fell away."

In a state of euphoria I left the cab. I had been given a delicious, unexpected dessert after a delicious, unexpected dinner.

73
Silence Gave Way to Song and It Was Spring

In 2018, Jody arranged for her and Nick to have an unveiling for their father's grave in Sag Harbor, a hundred miles from New York City. Nick agreed to come in from L.A., and since he and I had had that miraculous dinner together the previous summer, I thought maybe, since he had to pass through New York on his way home, he might follow up with a visit to me. I got no such invitation.

The unveiling took place on the holiest Shabbat in the Jewish calendar, the Shabbat between Rosh Hashanah and Yom Kippur. I was in shul, completely at ease with the fact Nick didn't call. It was okay; I had let it go. During the *amida* (silent prayer), another miracle. Spontaneously, I began praying to God to have the children forgive their father. Me, who years ago wanted not only that they hate him, but that they never forgive him. I imagined them singing and dancing around Phil's grave in a dance of forgiveness. And it made me happy.

I then found myself seeing Jody and Nick not only forgiving their father but *asking God to forgive him.*

I thought I had completed the journey after the dinner in L.A., but the subtle process of forgiveness I realized was ongoing. Each new moment I am showered with further understanding, I smile with a profound feeling of awe.

The following Tuesday I got a phone call from Hortencia, asking if she could she visit with me. She had some free time since Nick had freelance work to do in New York before leaving for home.

I invited her to the apartment for brunch and we spent three wonderful hours together. Saying goodbye, she asked for us to keep in touch by phone or email.

It was like spring, with tiny buds possibly becoming flowers. Sometimes it takes a lifetime for spring to come; sometimes it comes in another lifetime.

But for me spring arrived in autumn, at the beginning of the Jewish New Year 5778 quite unexpectedly and miraculously.

74
How Forgiveness Worked for Me

Without a Universal Power, a Higher All-Pervasive Consciousness, I never could have made this forgiveness journey.

Without forgiveness, I could have been weepy, sad, angry and self-righteous. Instead, I crawled up from the depths of despair, pain and betrayal to live a full, productive and meaningful life. I was able to forgive and be free. I live in awe and gratitude!

It not only took hard work, but courage, doggedness, and determination to change my life and fill it with joy instead of pain. However, I couldn't have done this without the help of a wise and talented therapist, my Guru, the teachings of my *zayde*, the Berditchever Rebbe, and God.

Or to put it another way, God blessed me by showering my life with the above mentioned gifts.

Hopefully, my story will inspire others to take the leap—and try to forgive.

Blessings on your journey, dear reader.

National Yiddish Book Center, Holyoke, Massachussetts, 1994

Baja California, 1995

Great Barrier Reef, Australia, 1996

Mexico, 1996

At photography exhibit in Modernage, New York City, 1997

Bhutan, 1997

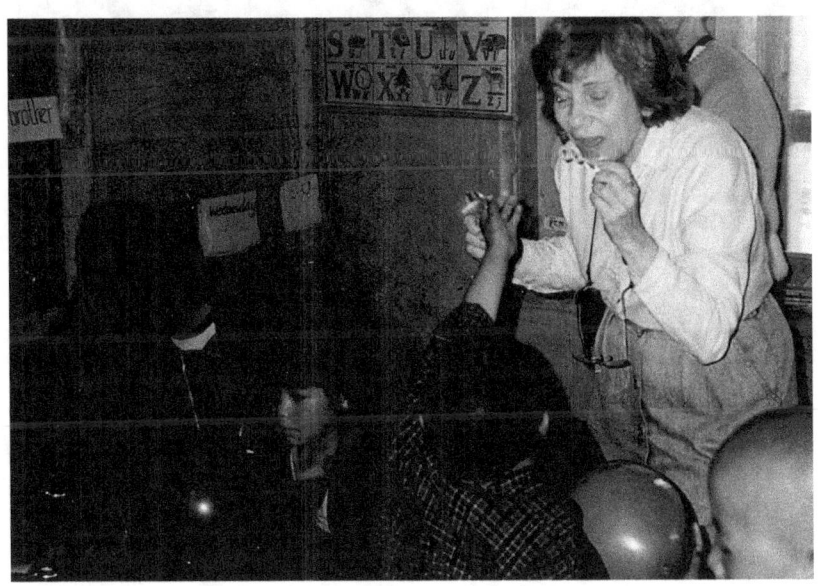

Delivering a letter from New York City in Llasa, Tibet, 1997

Traveling to a monastery in Bhutan, 1997

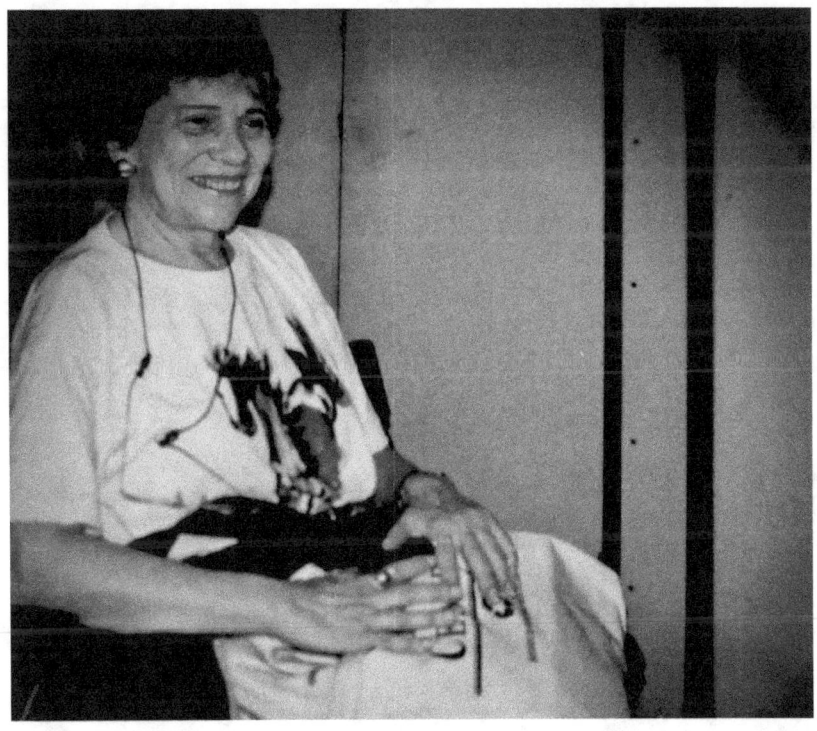

Hong Kong Ferry to Lantau, 1998

Scheyelle Islands, 1998

Evelyn & Marilyn's tent in Baja, California, 1999

With Samburu Tribe in Kenya, Africa, 1999

With Maasai Tribe in Tanzania, Africa, 1999

With Samburu Tribe in Kenya, Africa, 1999

Dancing with Aboriginal women in Darwin, Australia, 1999

Eating grubs in Australia, 1999

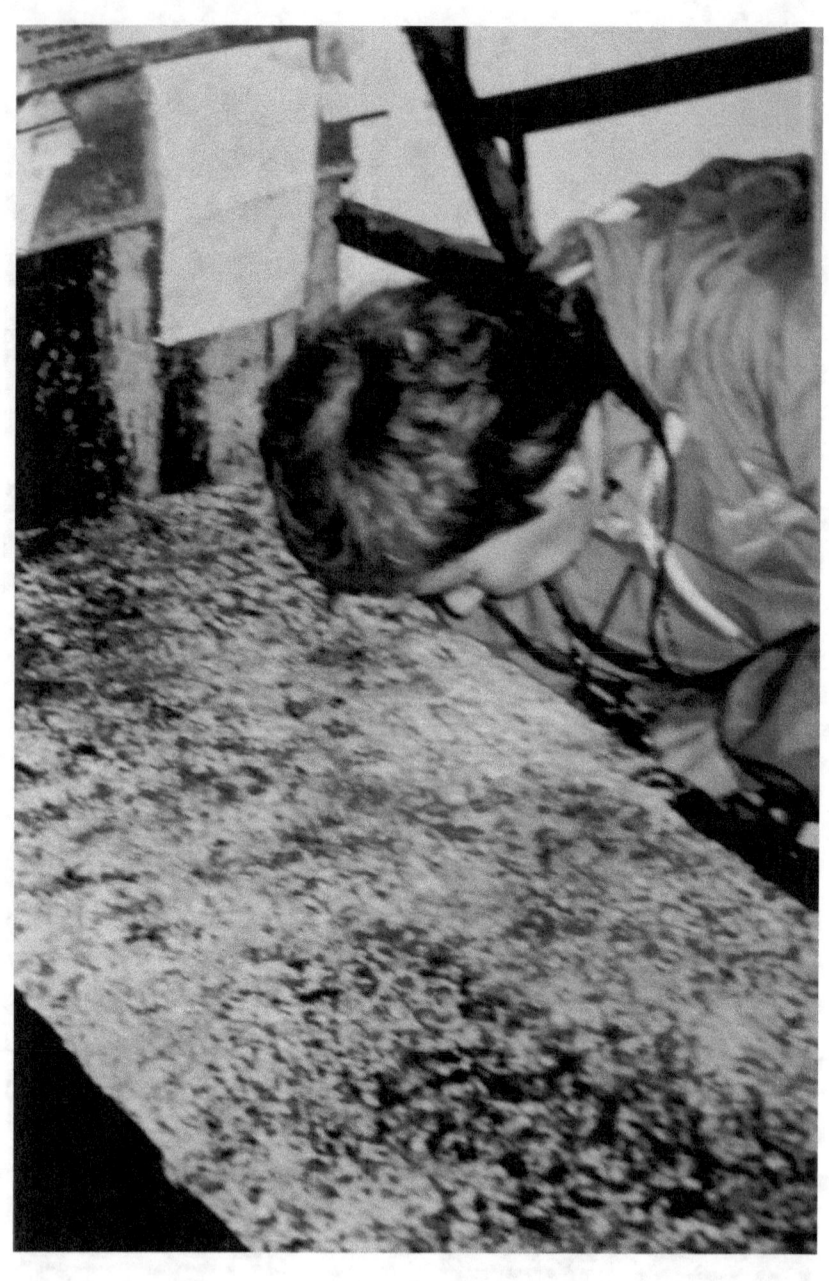

At Levi Yitzhak's grave in Berditchev, Ukraine, 2004

Swimming with dolphins in Key Largo, Florida, 2015

Evelyn in her apartment building lobby in New York City, 2017

90th birthday celebration at Romemu, New York City, June 2018

Jeff Elster & Evelyn at the New York Philharmonic, February 2020

Epilogue

I had known Evelyn since 1991, when we met at an ashram in India. Our connection was immediate. Over the years, we became closer and closer friends. In our conversations it often felt like sparks flew between us. When Evelyn called me in 2013 excited that she had started to write about her life, I offered to assist in typing up her handwritten notes and stories. Over the next seven years, we had nearly weekly phone calls, during which Evelyn read her latest writings, I typed, and we lovingly wrangled over words, punctuation, and edits.

Evelyn's memoir conveys the full depth and breadth of her journey. I believe her transparency was key to her healing and wholeness. The more she wrote, the more she found her true voice, rooted in conviction and clarity. Her writings help us see more of what is possible in the world, inside and out. When Evelyn was 91, even though her health had started to deteriorate, she made it a point to see places that she felt everyone should visit: she went with the SAJ on their Civil Rights Journey to the South to civil rights museums in Montgomery, Birmingham, and Atlanta. She had wanted to write about this important trip in her memoir but ran out of time. In her last month, Evelyn knew she had very little time and few moments of clarity left – and there were key edits she wanted to make. For one of the final edits, she added a sentence and emphasized that it would have an exclamation point. I double-checked. Evelyn replied enthusiastically, "Keep the exclamation point!" I realized this was the perfect metaphor for everything. It was Evelyn's dream to share this journey with the hope that perhaps it could inspire others. On her 92nd birthday, just one day before she passed, she was ecstatic to hold the first draft of the published book in her hands. This magical moment is captured in the photo below and was brought about by the enormous effort of the publisher, Penny Eifrig, who made Evelyn's dream come true after a serendipitous connection made by two of her dear friends, Barbara Siesel and Keith Torgan.

Evelyn's 40-year journey of forgiveness yielded liberation. Her freedom was hard-earned – she worked it from every angle – and it was filled with blessings. Evelyn's love of travel – which took her all over the world – was equaled only in her spirit of inner adventure. Evelyn spoke about death as her next journey...one without any baggage!

Her last word spoken was "Perfect."

~*Jeff Elster*

Evelyn's 92nd birthday with the first draft of her book,
June 19, 2020, one day before she departed on her final journey

Origin of the Back Cover Image

Almost 30 years ago I met Evelyn at a week-long program at the National Yiddish Book Center in Holyoke, Massachusetts. One Shabbat night that week at 4 o'clock in the morning, out of the blue I was awakened. Although I was alone in my room, I heard something or someone calling to me to open my heart and express my feelings about my Judaism. I got dressed and walked outside to collect my thoughts and was drawn to a secluded area with trees, shrubs, and a bench configured in a semi-circle. I sat down, closed my eyes, and suddenly an image appeared in my mind's eye as if it was familiar with me, like an old friend. The image was real, but it was not of this time or place. It was a small, shadowy figure, draped in a tallis, wearing a kippa, suspended in space, bathed in a soft radiant light which seemed to be emanating from its being. When I opened my eyes, the trees and the surroundings were illuminated with the soft light at sunrise through fog. I was inspired, my vision and this moment was a photographer's dream.

I knocked at Evelyn's door, holding a tallis, a kippah, and a prayerbook, explained my vision to Evelyn, and we quickly realized just how connected we were. We returned to that secluded area where together we created a dialogue which found its own voice. As we spoke, I walked around Evelyn, wearing the tallis and kippa and holding the prayerbook, in her meditative state. A window was opening and a divine presence was extending a hand and guiding me as I was recording all of my feelings and the experience on film. I found myself in an out-of-body experience flying in all directions, observing Evelyn's facial expressions and her responses to our dialogue. I continued to pray, to listen, to eavesdrop. I was in another dimension, another reality, riding a magic carpet through the cosmos. It was as if the pictures were taking themselves. I was inspired, frightened, amazed, and in awe of what was happening. For 45 minutes, I was in a different dimension with the most inspiring guide of my life. The encounter, the setting, the subject were a gift, a matana, from God. Evelyn was with me on every level for this entire experience, participating and creating with me. This began a most blessed journey of creating together for years the most profound life experiences in many different places and dimensions. No matter how lost we got, we always helped each other find our way.

~Marilyn Ellner, photographer, friend, and
traveling companion to Evelyn

Note from the Publisher:

I had the privilege of being introduced to Evelyn through two of Eifrig Publishing's children's book authors, Keith Torgan and Barbara Siesel, shortly before Evelyn passed. We had an inspired and intense conversation about her memoir project, her life and travels, and her final wishes to see her memoir published. In our conversation, she described a painting of a girl blowing dove-shaped bubbles and said that this was the image she wanted to have on the cover of her book. Evelyn had purchased the painting by Victor Jimenez Amaya which is replicated on the front cover at a street market in Mexico. I have not yet been able to reach the artist.

While she did not get to see the book with the final cover, within a week and on her 92nd birthday, she was able to hold a proof copy of her memoir and know that her journey of forgiveness would be shared with others.

I am grateful to have been able to share this special moment at the end of a "lifetime of radical amazement" with this remarkable woman.

~Penny Eifrig

www.ingramcontent.com/pod-product-compliance
Lightning Source LLC
Chambersburg PA
CBHW070442090526
44586CB00046B/1638